P9-DLZ-889

2

## Stand Out

# Grammar Challenge

THOMSON
*
HEINLE

Australia • Canada • Mexico • Singapore • Spain • United Kingdom • United States

**THOMSON**

**HEINLE**

## Stand Out 2
## Grammar Challenge

**Acquisitions Editor:** *Sherrise Roehr*
**Managing Editor:** *James W. Brown*
**Developmental Editor:** *Ingrid Wisniewska*
**Associate Developmental Editor:** *Sarah Barnicle*
**Editorial Assistant:** *Elizabeth Allen*
**Marketing Manager:** *Eric Bredenberg*
**Director, Global ESL Training & Development:** *Evelyn Nelson*
**Production Editor:** *Jeff Freeland*
**Senior Manufacturing Coordinator:** *Mary Beth Hennebury*
**Compositor:** *A Plus Publishing Services*
**Contributing Writer:** *Anita Raducanu*
**Printer:** *Victor Graphics, Inc.*

Copyright © 2002 Heinle, a division of Thomson Learning, Inc.
Thomson Learning™ is a trademark used herein under license.

Printed in the United States of America.
    7  8  9  10    06  05

For more information, contact Heinle, 25 Thomson Place, Boston, MA 02210 USA,
or you can visit our Internet site at http://www.heinle.com

All rights reserved. No part of this work covered by the copyright hereon may be reproduced
or used in any form or by any means—graphic, electronic, or mechanical, including
photocopying, recording, taping, Web distribution or information storage and retrieval
systems—without the written permission of the publisher.

For permission to use material from this text or product, contact us:
Tel      1-800-730-2214
Fax      1-800-730-2215
Web      www.thomsonrights.com

ISBN: 0-8384-3925-X

# TO THE TEACHER

*Stand Out Grammar Challenge 2* challenges students to develop and expand their grammar skills through sixty-four guided exercises or "challenges."

## Each Challenge includes:

▶ **Charts** Clear grammar charts help the teacher lay out the structure's components and provide useful example sentences.

▶ **Notes** Notes within the charts help students understand important shifts in language use and meaning through concise explanations.

▶ **Practice** Exercises challenge students to master grammar structures while reviewing the vocabulary and thematic contexts actively taught in *Stand Out Student Book 2*. Additional exercises reinforce grammar structures passively introduced in *Stand Out Student Book 2* contexts.

## How to use the *Stand Out Grammar Challenge 2* workbook

The *Stand Out Grammar Challenge 2* workbook can be used in a variety of ways:

- The grammar challenges can be assigned daily or on an as-needed basis.

- The grammar challenges can be completed individually, with a partner, or as a class.

- Students may complete challenges at home or in the classroom.

- Instructors can provide guided feedback upon completion, or ask students to self-correct or peer-edit. All exercises are formatted to provide for ease of correction and assessment.

- The *Grammar Challenge 2* answer key is available to teachers on the *Stand Out* web site at: **standout.heinle.com** It can be printed out for student use.

- The grammar challenges need not be followed in any particular order within a unit. Some challenges will be review for students, while others will reinforce the newer structures from *Stand Out Student Book 2*.

- The *Stand Out Grammar Challenge 2* workbook is an effective supplement in a multi-level classroom because it challenges the highly motivated students while providing support for students who need extra reinforcement.

The appendix includes a glossary of grammar terms with examples. This is intended as a reference for students and teachers, but it is not intended that all these terms will be understood at this level. The appendix also includes grammar charts from the *Stand Out Student Book 2* appendix as well as lists of irregular verbs and verb conjugations.

However you choose to use it, you'll find that the *Stand Out Grammar Challenge 2* workbook is a flexible and effective grammar tool for teachers and students seeking challenging grammar instruction.

# CONTENTS

**UNIT 1** **Everyday Life**

## CHALLENGE 1 ► Simple present of the verb *be*

| Full forms of *be* | | | Contracted forms |
|---|---|---|---|
| I | **am** | from Japan. | I**'m** from Japan. |
| You | **are** | tired. | You**'re** tired. |
| He, She, It | **is** | tall. | He**'s**, She**'s**, It**'s** tall. |
| We | **are** | busy. | We**'re** busy. |
| They | **are** | married. | They**'re** married. |

• In the contracted forms, the apostrophe (') shows that a letter is missing.
• Make contractions with subject pronouns in spoken and written language.
• Use contractions with names and things only in spoken language.
   **Kenji's** single.      My **sister's** married.

**A** Write the correct full form of the verb *be.*

EXAMPLES:    Kenji __*is*__ in Los Angeles.
                    He __*is*__ with his family.

1. Kenji's grandparents _are_ in Tokyo.
2. Marie _is_ in Palm City.
3. Anya and Ivan _are_ in Los Angeles, too.
4. You _are_ in Chicago today.
5. We _are_ at school.
6. On weekends, I _am_ with my mother.

7. In the summer, they _are_ in Brazil.
8. In the afternoon, we _are_ at work.
9. Lien _is_ at work, too.
10. Gilberto _is_ at the beach.
11. On Monday, I _am_ in English class.
12. You _are_ in English class, too.

**B** Rewrite each sentence using the contracted form of the verb *be.*

EXAMPLE:    My name is Mario.            ***My name's Mario.***

1. I am from Mexico.            I'm from Mexico.
2. She is from Guatemala.            She's from Guatemala.
3. We are married.            We're married.
4. Miguel is single.            Miguel's sigle.
5. He is short and thin.            He's short and thin.
6. It is sunny and warm today.            It's sunny and warm today.
7. At 7:00 P.M., I am in English class.            At 7:00 P.M., I'm in English class.
8. You are average height.            You're average height.
9. They are average weight.            They're average weight.
10. Lara is hungry and tired.            Lara's hungry and tired.

## CHALLENGE 2 ▶ Negative statements with the verb *be*

| Negative forms of *be* | | | Contracted forms | |
|---|---|---|---|---|
| I | **am not** | nervous. | **I'm not** | — |
| You | **are not** | in Houston. | you**'re not** | you **aren't** |
| He, She, It | **is not** | short. | he**'s**, she**'s**, it**'s not** | he, she, it **isn't** |
| We | **are not** | hungry. | we**'re not** | we **aren't** |
| They | **are not** | from Korea. | they**'re not** | they **aren't** |

- There is only one contracted form for **I am not: I'm not.**
- There are two contracted forms for the other negative forms of **be.**

**A** Choose the correct word(s) to complete each sentence. Mark the correct bubble. Fill in the bubble completely.

|  |  |  | **A** | **B** |
|---|---|---|---|---|
| EXAMPLE: I ___ at work on Monday. | A. isn't | B. am not | ○ | ● |
| 1. I ___ at school on Tuesday. | A. 'm not | B. 's not | ◉ | ○ |
| 2. It ___ sunny this afternoon. | A. 're not | B. 's not | ○ | ◉ |
| 3. It ___ very warm either. | A. isn't | B. aren't | ○ | ○ |
| 4. My friends ___ at the beach today. | A. are not | B. is not | ○ | ○ |
| 5. They ___ happy about the weather. | A. isn't | B. aren't | ○ | ○ |
| 6. We ___ always busy. | A. 's not | B. 're not | ○ | ○ |
| 7. We ___ tired either. | A. are not | B. am not | ○ | ○ |
| 8. My friend Mario ___ single. | A. is not | B. are not | ○ | ○ |
| 9. My friend Lien ___ married. | A. 're not | B. 's not | ○ | ○ |
| 10. You ___ married either. | A. aren't | B. isn't | ○ | ○ |

**B** Use the words in parentheses and make each sentence negative. Use a contraction.

EXAMPLE: My name's Gilberto. (Antonio)   *My name isn't Antonio.*

1. I'm from Brazil. (Portugal) _____

2. I'm married. (single) _____

3. His name is Fernando. (Roberto) _____

4. Her name is Rosa. (Ella) _____

5. We're tall and thin. (small) _____

6. My parents are Augustín and Sylvia. (Ramon and Bianca) _____

7. You're in their restaurant. (house) _____

8. It's warm today. (cold) _____

**UNIT 1** Everyday Life

## CHALLENGE 3 ► Questions with the verb *be*

| Yes/no questions |
| --- |
| **Am I** happy? |
| **Are you** married? |
| **Is he** tall? |
| **Is she** from Haiti? |
| **Is it** sunny today? |
| **Are we** friends? |
| **Are they** in class? |

| Wh- questions | |
| --- | --- |
| **Who** is from Japan? | **Who** are your brothers? |
| **What** is your name? | **What** are their names? |
| **When** is your English class? | **When** am I busy? |
| **Why** is Gilberto always busy? | **Why** are we nervous? |
| **Where** is my sister? | **Where** are you from? |
| **How** is the weather today? | **How** are you today? |

• The verb **be** can contract with **wh-** words: **who's, what's when's, why's, how's.**

**A** Use the words to ask a *yes/no* question.

EXAMPLE:   Kenji / from Japan     ___*Is Kenji from Japan?*_____

1.  Anya and Ivan / from Russia   _____
2.  you / from Korea   _____
3.  I / late for class   _____
4.  Marie / from Haiti   _____
5.  we / busy today   _____
6.  Gilberto and Mario / tall   _____
7.  Mario / from Mexico   _____
8.  Kenji / at school   _____

**B** Read each answer (A) below. Then complete the question (Q) with the correct *wh-* question word + a form of *be.*

EXAMPLE:   Q: ___*Where is*_____ Kenji from?   A: Kenji is from Japan.

1.  Q: _____ his sister's name?   A: His sister's name is Miyuki.
2.  Q: _____ his brothers' names?   A: His brothers' names are Genki and Akira.
3.  Q: _____ Kenji's parents?   A: Kenji's parents are Ayumi and Takuya.
4.  Q: _____ his grandparents?   A: His grandparents are in Japan.
5.  Q: _____ Kenji in English class?   A: Kenji is in English class on Tuesday.
6.  Q: _____ Kenji's English class?   A: Kenji's English class is in the high school.
7.  Q: _____ Kenji's teacher?   A: Kenji's teacher is Mr. Brown.
8.  Q: _____ Kenji today?   A: Kenji is happy.
9.  Q: _____ Kenji happy?   A: Because he is going to the beach.
10. Q: _____ the weather today?   A: It is sunny and warm.

## CHALLENGE 4 ▶ Indefinite and definite articles with singular nouns

| Indefinite articles | Definite article |
|---|---|
| I am **a** cook. <br> He has **an** aunt in Japan. | **The** teacher is busy. <br> Is **the** weather rainy in Florida? |

- Use **a** for nouns that start with a consonant: **a** bus.
- Use **an** for nouns that start with a vowel: **an** aunt.
- Use **a** or **an** for general things or for introducing a singular noun.
- Use **the** for specific things or for something already mentioned.

**A** Insert *a* or *an* in the correct place.

EXAMPLE:  Lien is ^*a* friend.

1.  She is from city in Vietnam.

2.  She has aunt in San Diego.

3.  She has uncle in Los Angeles.

4.  She has cousin in Los Angeles, too.

5.  Her brother is cook.

6.  Lien is student at Oakhill College.

7.  She has English class on Monday.

8.  She has teacher from Boston.

9.  There is clock in the classroom.

10.  There is map, too.

**B** Complete the sentences with *a, an,* or *the.*

EXAMPLE:  I have __*a*__ friend named Gilberto.

1.  He lives in _____ United States.

2.  He has _____ aunt and _____ uncle who live in Brazil.

3.  Gilberto is _____ cook in his father's restaurant.

4.  _____ restaurant has American food.

5.  Gilberto has _____ wife. Her name is Teresa.

6.  They have two children— _____ son and _____ daughter.

7.  _____ boy's name is José, and _____ girl's name is Olivia.

8.  Gilberto often takes _____ children to school.

9.  On Saturday, _____ family goes to the beach.

10.  _____ beach is wonderful.

# UNIT 1 Everyday Life

## CHALLENGE 5 ▶ Simple present of the verb *have*

| | *have* | |
|---|---|---|
| I | **have** | two sisters. |
| You | **have** | blond hair. |
| He, She, It | **has** | brown eyes. |
| We | **have** | English class in the morning. |
| They | **have** | blue notebooks. |

 **A** Circle the correct word to complete each sentence.

EXAMPLE:   My friend Kenji (has)/ have black hair.

1.  He  has / have  brown eyes.

2.  Kenji's sister Yakari  has / have  brown eyes.

3.  His brothers  has / have  brown eyes, too.

4.  My sister Patricia  has / have  blue eyes.

5.  My parents  has / have brown eyes.

6.  I  has / have  green eyes.

7.  We all  has / have  brown hair.

8.  Do you  has / have  brown hair, too?

9.  I  has / have  a dog.

10. It  has / have  big brown eyes.

**B** Complete the description of Anya and her family with the correct forms of the verb *have*.

Anya is from Moscow, Russia. She is average height and weight. She (1) _____ gray hair and brown eyes. She lives in Los Angeles with her husband Ivan. Ivan (2) _____ brown eyes and he is nearly bald.  Anya and Ivan (3) _____ two children, Irina and Dimitri. Irina (4) _____ one child. Dimitri (5) _____ two children. The grandchildren always say, "We (6) _____ wonderful grandparents."

Today is Monday. Ivan asks Anya, "Do you (7) _____ English class today?" Anya says, "Yes, I (8) _____ class at 7:00 P.M. There are fifteen students in the class. We (9) _____ a very good teacher. He always (10) _____ time for our questions."

## CHALLENGE 6 ► Negative statements with the verb *have*

| Negative forms of *have* | | | Contracted forms |
|---|---|---|---|
| I | **do not have** | English class today. | I **don't have** |
| You | **do not have** | a telephone. | you **don't have** |
| He, She, It | **does not have** | brown eyes. | he, she, it **doesn't have** |
| We | **do not have** | three children. | we **don't have** |
| They | **do not have** | many friends. | they **don't have** |

**A** Circle the correct sentence.

EXAMPLE: (My sister does not have children.) / My sister do not have children.

1. I does not have a wife. / I do not have a wife.
2. We does not have many friends in New York. / We do not have many friends in New York.
3. You do not have an aunt in Korea. / You does not have an aunt in Korea.
4. They do not have uncles in the U.S. / They does not have uncles in the U.S.
5. Ken do not have a brother. / Ken does not have a brother.
6. My mother does not have a sister. / My mother do not have a sister.
7. You doesn't have a niece in Poland. / You don't have a niece in Poland.
8. Maria don't have a husband. / Maria doesn't have a husband.
9. I don't have many friends. / I doesn't have many friends.
10. My aunt and uncle doesn't have children. / My aunt and uncle don't have children.

**B** Complete each sentence with the negative form of *have*. Use a contraction.

EXAMPLE: Paulo __*doesn't have*__ English class in the morning.

1. We _____ class in the afternoon.
2. He _____ English class at 7:00 P.M.
3. I _____ many Japanese students in my English class.
4. My friends _____ a new English teacher.
5. Lien _____ twenty students in her class.
6. They _____ many friends in the class.
7. The teacher _____ a calendar on the wall.
8. She _____ a picture on the wall.
9. The students _____ many questions.
10. You _____ free time after class.

**UNIT 1**  **Everyday Life**

## CHALLENGE 7 ► Questions with the verb *have*

| Yes/no question | Short answer | |
|---|---|---|
| **Do** I (you, we, they) **have** children? | Yes, I (you, we, they) **do.** | No, I (you, we, they) **don't.** |
| **Does** he (she, it) **have** a clock? | Yes, he (she, it) **does.** | No, he (she, it) **doesn't.** |
| **Wh-** question | Answer | |
| **Who** do I **have** for an English teacher? | You **have** Mr. Townsend. | |
| **What** do you **have** for breakfast? | I **have** coffee and toast. | |
| **When** does he **have** free time? | He **has** free time on Monday afternoon. | |
| **Where** do we **have** class today? | We **have** class in room 34. | |
| **How many** brothers do they **have**? | They **have** two brothers. | |

**A** Ask if these people have the items. Then give the answer.

EXAMPLE:   Mario / a clock (yes)   ___*Does Mario have a clock?*___   ___*Yes, he does.*___

1.  Anya and Ivan / a car (no)   _____   _____

2.  you / a picture of Moscow (yes)   _____   _____

3.  I / your phone number (no)   _____   _____

4.  Irina / a thermometer (no)   _____   _____

5.  they / a telephone (yes)   _____   _____

6.  Alexi / a soccer ball (yes)   _____   _____

7.  it / the weather report (no)   _____   _____

8.  we / a map of Portland (yes)   _____   _____

**B** Unscramble the words to form *wh-* questions.

EXAMPLE:   have / how many / does / children / she   ___*How many children does she have?*___

1.  you / when / have / do / English class   _____

2.  why / have / he / free time / does   _____

3.  for breakfast / do / what / we / have   _____

4.  today / Kenji / does / have / class / when   _____

5.  have / do / who / I / in my class   _____

6.  go / she / does / where / to school   _____

7.  have / how many / you / aunts / do   _____

8.  do / you / a map / why / have   _____

9.  for a teacher / we / have / who / do   _____

10.  have / when / they / the weather report / do   _____

Simple present and frequency words

## CHALLENGE 8 ► Simple present and frequency words

| | work | | | go | |
|---|---|---|---|---|---|
| I | **work** | in the morning. | I | **go** | to school. |
| You | **work** | in the afternoon. | You | **go** | to the beach. |
| He, She, It | **work<u>s</u>** | at 6 A.M. | He, She, It | **go<u>es</u>** | with the children. |
| We | **work** | on Saturday. | We | **go** | to Florida in the winter. |
| They | **work** | with my sister. | They | **go** | to class on Tuesday. |

• Frequency words tell how often something happens.

FREQUENCY WORD: **never   rarely   sometimes   often   always**

FREQUENCY: 0% ◄————————————————► 100%

• Most of the time, frequency words come before the verb form: We **never** work on Sunday.

• With the verb **be,** frequency words come after the verb form: I am **often** busy on Monday.

**A** Rewrite each sentence with the new subject in parentheses.

EXAMPLE:   I wake up at 6:00 A.M. (Anya)      *Anya wakes up at 6:00 A.M.* _____

1. Ivan gets up at 7:00 A.M. (you)          _____

2. We go to work at 8:00 A.M. (Ivan)       _____

3. They are always busy in the afternoon. (it)  _____

4. Anya helps with the grandchildren. (they)  _____

5. Vladimir and Ziven play soccer. (we)     _____

6. You work in Los Angeles. (Ivan)          _____

7. The children go to school. (I)           _____

8. I take the children to the beach. (Anya)  _____

**B** Complete each sentence with the verb and frequency word in parentheses.

EXAMPLE:   (wake up / often) Gilberto __*often wakes up*__ at 5:00 A.M.

1. (work / always) He _____ at his father's restaurant.

2. (take / sometimes) His children _____ the bus to school.

3. (play / often) His friends _____ soccer on Sunday.

4. (be / never) His sister Rosa _____ busy on Saturday.

5. (work / sometimes) On Mondays, she _____ overtime.

6. (get up / rarely) I _____ up at 6:00 A.M.

7. (be / never) I _____ late for work.

8. (wake up / sometimes) My brother _____ at 7:00 A.M.

9. (take / rarely) We _____ the bus to work.

10. (come / often) It _____ late.

# Time to Go Shopping

## CHALLENGE 1 ▶ Negative simple present

| Subject | do + not | Base | Example |
|---------|----------|------|---------|
| I<br>You<br>We<br>They | do not<br>(don't) | wear<br>shop<br>work<br>like | I don't wear jeans to work. |
| He, She, It | does not<br>(doesn't) | eat<br>need | He doesn't eat pizza. |

**A** **Rewrite each sentence using the contracted form.**

EXAMPLE:   Aminata <u>does not wear</u> jeans to school.     <u>**Aminata doesn't wear jeans to school.**</u>

1.  I <u>do not wear</u> a tie to work. _____

2.  Marie <u>does not wear</u> sandals in the summer. _____

3.  We <u>do not wear</u> boots to work. _____

4.  Pablo <u>does not wear</u> gloves in the winter. _____

5.  You <u>do not wear</u> socks with your sneakers. _____

6.  My friends <u>do not wear</u> T-shirts to school. _____

7.  I <u>do not wear</u> a hat in the summer. _____

8.  My dog <u>does not wear</u> a sweater in the winter. _____

9.  Irina <u>does not wear</u> shorts to the mall. _____

10.  They <u>do not wear</u> backpacks to school. _____

**B** **Complete the sentences with the negative form of the underlined verb.**

EXAMPLE:   Kenji <u>shops</u> at Bayview Mall. He __<u>**doesn't shop**</u>__ at Maple Lake Mall.

1.  Marie <u>wears</u> sandals to the beach. She _____ sandals to work.

2.  I <u>need</u> jeans for my work. I _____ a suit for my work.

3.  You <u>buy</u> shoes at Allen's Shoe Store. You _____ shoes at The Shoe Place.

4.  My parents <u>like</u> the new mall. They _____ the old mall.

5.  Ivan <u>needs</u> new boots. He _____ new shoes.

6.  You often <u>shop</u> on Saturday. You _____ on Sunday.

7.  After shopping, we always <u>eat</u> in the mall. We _____ at home.

8.  Tan and Diem <u>want</u> new summer clothes. They _____ new winter clothes.

9.  I <u>work</u> in a small store. I _____ in a department store.

10.  The ad <u>says</u> the dress is $40. It _____ the dress is $50.

**Yes/no questions with simple present**

## CHALLENGE 2 ▶ *Yes/no* questions with simple present

| Yes/no question | | | Short answer | |
|---|---|---|---|---|
| **Do** | I | **need** a coat? | Yes, you **do.** | No, you **don't.** |
| | you | | Yes, I **do.** | No, I **don't.** |
| | we | | Yes, we **do.** | No, we **don't.** |
| | they | | Yes, they **do.** | No, they **don't.** |
| **Does** | he | **wear** sweaters? | Yes, he **does.** | No, he **doesn't.** |
| | she | | Yes, she **does.** | No, she **doesn't.** |
| | it | | Yes, it **does.** | No, it **doesn't.** |

- Use **do** with **I, you, we, they,** and plural subjects.
- Use **does** with **he, she, it,** and singular subjects.
- Always use the base form after **do** or **does.**

**A** Read each statement. Write a *yes/no* question using that statement.

EXAMPLE:  You like my shoes.     *Do you like my shoes?*

1. They cost $45.00. _____
2. The price includes tax. _____
3. You shop at the mall. _____
4. Kenji shops there, too. _____
5. We want to buy new clothes. _____
6. I need more money. _____
7. Mr. Lee has a new raincoat. _____
8. Silvia wears sandals every day. _____

**B** Answer each question according to the information in parentheses.

EXAMPLE:   Does Lien wear boots in the winter? (yes)     *Yes, she does.*

1. Do you use coupons? (yes) _____
2. Does the ad give the regular price? (no) _____
3. Does Addy's Clothing Store have good prices? (yes) _____
4. Do Mario and Teresa shop at Addy's Clothing Store? (no) _____
5. Do we have $75.00 for the coat? (no) _____
6. Does the price include tax? (yes) _____
7. Do I need a coat today? (yes) _____
8. Does Alexi buy cheap shoes? (no) _____
9. Do you have $25.00? (no) _____
10. Does your mother need a new hat? (yes) _____

## CHALLENGE 3  ▶ *Wh-* questions with simple present

| *Wh-* question | | | | Answer |
|---|---|---|---|---|
| **Who** | **do** | **I** | **take** to the mall today? | You take your sister. |
| **What** | | you | **need** at the store? | I need some jeans. |
| **Where** | | we | **eat** lunch? | We eat at Pizza Palace. |
| **How** | | they | **get** to the mall? | They get to the mall by bus. |
| **When** | **does** | he | **shop** on Saturday? | He shops in the afternoon. |
| **Why** | | she | **wear** shorts to work? | She wears shorts because it's hot. |

• Note also:  **how much**    **How much** do they cost?
              **how many**    **How many shirts** do you have?

 **A**   **Circle the correct word to complete each sentence.**

EXAMPLE:   Why (do)/ does you like the red shoes?

1.  Where do / does you shop?
2.  Where do /does Yuko shop?
3.  How do / does you get to the mall?
4.  What do / does Tia wear with her blue shirt?
5.  How many coupons do / does they have?

6.  Who do / does I get coupons from?
7.  When do / does we use the coupons?
8.  What do / does the advertisement say?
9.  How much money do / does we have?
10. Why do / docs the price include tax?

**B**   **Unscramble the words to write *wh-* questions in the simple present.**

EXAMPLE:   they / where / shoes / buy / do        *Where do they buy shoes?*

1.  do / how many / need / we / shirts       _____
2.  do / find / a coupon / I / where         _____
3.  Mario / to / does / wear / what / work   _____
4.  cost / how much / do / the sneakers      _____
5.  when / the dog / does / wear / a sweater _____
6.  you / $35.00 / do / why / want           _____
7.  shop / with / who / you / do             _____
8.  does / shop / Irina / when               _____
9.  want / to buy / what / do / they         _____
10. do / how much / save / we                _____

**Possessive adjectives**

## CHALLENGE 4 ▸ Possessive adjectives

| Subject pronoun | Possessive adjective | Example |
|---|---|---|
| I | my | I shop every Saturday with **my** mother. |
| you | your | You and **your** sister need new shoes. |
| he | his | He buys **his** dog a new sweater every year. |
| she | her | She takes **her** father to the store in the morning. |
| it | its | Is that your dog? **Its** sweater is very nice. |
| we | our | We shop with **our** family at the Milltown Mall. |
| they | their | **Their** favorite department store is Anderson's. |

**A** Complete each sentence with the possessive adjective that refers to the subject.

EXAMPLE:   Steve likes ___*his*___ new hat.

1. She wears _____ jeans to work.

2. You buy all _____ clothes at Porter's.

3. I shop for _____ clothes at The Boutique.

4. The cat wears _____ sweater all the time.

5. We need _____ coats in the winter.

6. Mario and _____ family often wear shorts.

7. They use _____ coupons to buy clothes.

8. The children wear _____ T-shirts to school.

9. You never wear _____ hat in the summer.

10. I don't have _____ receipt from the store.

**B** Choose the correct word to complete each sentence. Mark the correct bubble. Fill in the bubble completely.

|  |  |  | A | B |
|---|---|---|---|---|
| EXAMPLE:   I like ___ striped shirt. | A. we | B. my | ○ | ● |
| 1. Lien wants ___ plaid jacket. | A. she | B. her | ○ | ○ |
| 2. Where do they buy ___ shoes? | A. their | B. he | ○ | ○ |
| 3. You always wear a green shirt with ___ brown pants. | A. your | B. its | ○ | ○ |
| 4. Vladimir and Ziven wear ___ blue backpacks to school. | A. they | B. their | ○ | ○ |
| 5. We don't wear ___ expensive shoes to the beach. | A. our | B. you | ○ | ○ |
| 6. When it snows, the dog wears ___ flowered sweater. | A. its | B. it | ○ | ○ |
| 7. It's rainy today. I need ___ raincoat. | A. its | B. my | ○ | ○ |
| 8. The dress is $20.00 off ___ regular price. | A. its | B. her | ○ | ○ |
| 9. We always buy ___ winter clothes at the mall. | A. we | B. our | ○ | ○ |
| 10. Kenji never wears ___ red tie. | A. he | B. his | ○ | ○ |
| 11. Do you want ___ shorts and T-shirt? | A. your | B. you | ○ | ○ |
| 12. Does Marie wear ___ scarf in the winter? | A. she | B. her | ○ | ○ |

**UNIT 2**

# Time to Go Shopping

## CHALLENGE 5 ► Present continuous

| Subject | *be* | Base verb + *ing* | Example |
|---------|------|-------------------|---------|
| I | am | wearing | I **am wearing** my flowered shirt today. |
| You | are | buying | You **are buying** a new hat. |
| He, She, It | is | wearing | He **is**, She **is**, It **is wearing** a sweater. |
| We | are | going | We **are going** to the mall right now. |
| They | are | shopping | They **are shopping** with their aunt. |

- For most verbs, add **-ing** to the base: eat**ing**, study**ing**.
- For one-syllable verbs ending in *consonant + vowel + consonant,* double the final consonant and add **-ing**: shop**ping**, plan**ning**.
- For verbs ending in *consonant +* **e,** drop the **e** and add **-ing**: tak**ing**.
- You can make a contraction with the subject and a form of **be.**
  **I'm** wearing new shoes.          **Tan's** wearing a new coat.
- To form the negative, put **not** after the form of **be.**
  **I'm not** buying a new shirt.          Anya **isn't** shopping today.

**A** Fill in the missing part of each sentence.

EXAMPLES:   It's rain **_ing_** today.
                   I **_am_** going to the mall.

1. You _____ going to the mall with me.
2. Marie isn't work_____ today.
3. She _____ going with us.
4. I'm wear_____ my raincoat.
5. We _____ wearing hats, too.

6. Anya and Ivan _____ shopping today, too.
7. They'_____ buying winter clothes.
8. Mario _____ working today.
9. His wife, Teresa, is work_____, too.
10. They _____n't going to the mall.

**B** Use the words to write a sentence in the present continuous.

EXAMPLE:   many people / shop / today          ___*Many people are shopping today.*___

1. Anya / look / for new summer clothes _____
2. I / buy / sandals _____
3. you / wear / your new blouse _____
4. three men / sit / on a bench _____
5. we / not / eat / at the mall today _____
6. Duong / go / to the shoe store _____
7. the children / talk / to their friends _____
8. Irina / not / buy the blue skirt _____
9. you / read / a book at the bookstore _____
10. we / take / the bus home _____

## CHALLENGE 6 ▶ *Yes/no* questions with present continuous

| *be* | Subject | Base verb + *ing* | Short answer | |
|------|---------|-------------------|--------------|---|
| Am | I | **going** with you to the mall? | Yes, you **are**. | No, you **aren't**. |
| Are | you | **shopping** today? | Yes, I **am**. | No, I **'m not**. |
| Is | he, she, it | **wearing** a sweater? | Yes, he, she, it **is**. | No, he, she, it **isn't**. |
| Are | we | **buying** new jeans now? | Yes, we **are**. | No, we **aren't**. |
| Are | they | **having** a sale right now? | Yes, they **are**. | No, they **aren't**. |

- To form a negative question, use a contraction with **not** after the form of **be**.
  **aren't you, isn't he, isn't she, isn't it, aren't we, aren't they**
- For the subject pronoun **I**, use **aren't I** to make a negative question.

### A Ask *yes/no* questions about what these people are buying.

EXAMPLE:   Diem / the striped shirt        *Is Diem buying the striped shirt?* _____

1. Anya and Ivan / summer clothes        _____
2. you / the blue pants or the red pants   _____
3. I / the dress with a coupon           _____
4. Teresa / the flowered raincoat        _____
5. we / the extra-large T-shirts         _____
6. they / expensive shoes                _____
7. Steve / the brown boots               _____
8. your family / winter clothes today    _____

### B Answer each question according to the information in parentheses.

EXAMPLE:   Is he using a discount coupon? (yes)        *Yes, he is.* _____

1. Are they looking at the clothing in a flyer? (yes)    _____
2. Is he saving $10 with the coupon? (no)                _____
3. Aren't you buying the skirt for $39.95? (yes)         _____
4. Is Lien buying the dress at the regular price? (no)   _____
5. Aren't I saving $5 with the coupon? (no)              _____
6. Aren't we taking the receipt? (yes)                   _____
7. Are the children buying new backpacks? (yes)          _____
8. Are you reading the advertisement? (no)               _____
9. Am I shopping with you today? (yes)                   _____
10. Is So talking about the clothing prices? (no)        _____

# Time to Go Shopping

## CHALLENGE 7 ► *Wh-* questions with present continuous

| Wh- word | be | Subject | Base verb + *ing* | Example |
|---|---|---|---|---|
| **Who** | **am** | I | **taking** | **Who am** I **taking** to the mall? |
| **Where** | **are** | you | **going** | **Where are** you **going** now? |
| **What** | **is** | he, she, it | **wearing** | **What is** he, she, it **wearing**? |
| **When** | **are** | we | **buying** | **When are** we **buying** new clothes? |
| **Why** | **are** | they | **shopping** | **Why are** they **shopping** today? |

- To form the negative, use a contraction with **not** after the form of **be**.
  **aren't you, isn't he, isn't she, isn't it, aren't we, aren't they**
- For the subject pronoun **I**, use **aren't I**.

 **Find the mistake in each sentence and correct it.**

EXAMPLES:   Why ~~are~~ **is** she buying a new dress?
    What are you ~~look~~ **looking** at in the flyer?

1.  Where is we going today?
2.  Who is Kenji go to the mall with?
3.  Why are he using a coupon?
4.  How am you going to the mall?
5.  What are you wear with your new skirt?

6.  When is they shopping for summer clothes?
7.  Why aren't you buy the blue jacket?
8.  What are the dog wearing?
9.  How much is I saving?
10.  Why aren't she taking the receipt?

**B** **Unscramble the words to form questions.**

EXAMPLE:   is / today / Lara / where / going    **_Where is Lara going today?_**

1.  going / is / she / how / to the mall    _____
2.  the children / wearing / are / what    _____
3.  going / we / are / when / to the mall    _____
4.  with you / you / taking / who / are    _____
5.  why / wearing / Franco / isn't / sandals    _____
6.  where / today / we / eating / lunch / are    _____
7.  is / a raincoat / your sister / buying / when    _____
8.  reading / you / are / what    _____
9.  where / shoes / Tan and Diem / are / buying    _____
10.  to the store / I / taking / who / am    _____

## CHALLENGE 8 ▶ Present continuous and simple present

| **Present continuous** |
|---|
| The present continuous is used with **now, right now, at the (this) moment, today.**<br>    Diem **is buying** a new scarf **right now.** |
| **Simple present** |
| The simple present is used with **always, often, usually, never, sometimes,**<br>**every day/month/season.**<br>    He **buys** one **every winter.** |

**A** Complete each sentence with the present continuous or simple present.

EXAMPLE: (wait) Duong _____*is waiting*_____ for his sister outside the department store right now.

1. (go) They usually _____ to the Mountain View Mall on their lunch break.
2. (eat) Today they _____ pizza for lunch.
3. (shop) Lien _____ for a blue skirt at this moment.
4. (buy) She never _____ jeans because she doesn't like them.
5. (look) Sometimes Anya _____ for new clothes, but not often.
6. (wear) Mario and his family always _____ warm clothes in January.
7. (spend) Irina and Alexis usually _____ too much money for clothes.
8. (walk) At the moment, we _____ around J. D. Allen's Department Store.
9. (get) I often _____ tired because I hate shopping.
10. (need) Every summer you _____ a new pair of sandals.

**B** Complete each sentence with the present continuous or simple present of a verb from the box. Some verbs are used more than once.

| have | buy | go | shop | look | wear | talk | save |
|---|---|---|---|---|---|---|---|

EXAMPLE: I always _____*wear*_____ jeans to work.

1. I usually _____ my jeans at J. D. Allen's Department Store.
2. Every Monday they _____ a big sale.
3. My sister needs jeans, too. We _____ to the mall right now.
4. The Nguyen brothers _____ at the mall today, too.
5. At the moment, they _____ for new sneakers and boots.
6. Sam's Uniform Company _____ a sale on shirts and shoes today.
7. Sam's always _____ good sale prices.
8. Duong _____ to a salesperson now.
9. Today, they _____ their new sneakers and boots with a coupon.
10. With a coupon, you sometimes _____ $10 off the regular price.

# UNIT 3 — Food and Nutrition

## CHALLENGE 1 ► Review: Negative simple present

| Subject | *do + not* | Base | |
|---------|-----------|------|---|
| I | **don't** | like | french fries. |
| You | **don't** | order | pizza for lunch. |
| He, She, It | **doesn't** | eat | He doesn't eat tuna fish for lunch. |
| We | **don't** | need | orange juice. |
| They | **don't** | have | cheesecake today. |

• Remember: **don't** is the contraction for **do not**; **doesn't** is the contraction for **does not.**

 **A**  If the sentence is affirmative, make it negative. If it is negative, make it affirmative.

EXAMPLES:  We <u>like</u> chocolate cake.  ___*We don't like chocolate cake.*___

Mrs. Kim <u>doesn't need</u> water.  ___*Mrs. Kim needs water.*___

1. Ana <u>works</u> in a restaurant.  _____
2. You <u>don't order</u> a salad every day.  _____
3. We <u>don't want</u> rice with our beef.  _____
4. All main courses <u>come</u> with soup.  _____
5. I <u>don't eat</u> lunch here on Saturday.  _____
6. Diem <u>doesn't like</u> the fried noodles.  _____
7. They <u>have</u> good coffee here.  _____
8. We <u>don't need</u> dessert.  _____
9. You <u>want</u> a side order of beans.  _____
10. His dog <u>doesn't eat</u> pepperoni pizza.  _____

**B**  Answer the questions in the negative.

EXAMPLE:  Does Pablo like vegetables?  ___*No, he doesn't like vegetables.*___

1. Does Gabriela eat fish?  _____
2. Do you buy eggs every day?  _____
3. Does Kenji have soup for lunch?  _____
4. Do Anya and Ivan like Caesar salad?  _____
5. Do we need a loaf of bread?  _____
6. Does the dog like tuna fish?  _____
7. Do I need sugar for a balanced diet?  _____
8. Do you want pickles with the hamburger?  _____
9. Do they have chicken today?  _____
10. Does Mr. Brown order soup for lunch?  _____

# Food and Nutrition

## CHALLENGE 2 ► Count and non-count nouns

| Count nouns |
| --- |
| Count nouns are nouns that can be counted. They have a singular and a plural form. |
| **a restaurant, two restaurants; one orange, six oranges; one pancake, three pancakes** |

| Non-count nouns |
| --- |
| Non-count nouns cannot be counted. They only have a singular form. |
| They are nouns from one of the following groups: |

- nouns with no individual/single parts: **milk, soup, meat, butter, jelly**
- nouns with parts that are too small to count: **rice, sugar, corn, flour**
- nouns that mean a group of things: **food, money, clothing**
- nouns that are ideas: **nutrition, health, time, work, education**

**A** Label each word as *count* or *non-count.*

EXAMPLE:  water  **_non-count_**

1. vegetables _____
2. spaghetti _____
3. onion _____
4. jars _____
5. beef _____
6. donut _____

7. sugar _____
8. cookies _____
9. water _____
10. apple _____
11. drinks _____
12. potatoes _____

**B** Circle the correct form of the underlined word.

EXAMPLE:  Bread is made from (flour)/ flours.

1. I need to buy three pizza / pizzas.
2. Do you want water / waters with your meal?
3. Gilberto is making soup / soups.
4. You are making sandwich / sandwiches for 20 people.
5. Silvia always eats tomato / tomatoes with her dinner.
6. We are tired of this food / foods.
7. I'll have two baked potato / potatoes, please.
8. Where are the cake mix / cake mixes?
9. Good nutrition / nutritions is important.
10. There are six food group /groups in the nutrition pyramid.

## CHALLENGE 3 ▸ *A lot of, many, much, a few, a little*

| a lot of, many, much, a few, a little | |
|---|---|
| **COUNT (PLURAL)** | **NON-COUNT** |
| He eats **many/a lot of** cookies. | He eats **a lot of** rice. |
| He doesn't eat **many/a lot of** cookies. | He doesn't eat **much/a lot of** rice. |
| Does he eat **many/a lot of** cookies? | Does he each **much/a lot of** rice? |
| **How many** cookies does he eat? | **How much** rice does he eat? |
| He has **a few** cookies. | He has **a little** rice. |

- **A lot of, many,** and **much** are used to show a large quantity.
- **Much** is rarely used in affirmative statements with non-count nouns. Use **a lot of.**
- **A few** and **a little** are used to show a small quantity.

**A**  Complete the sentences with *a lot of, many,* or *much.* Sometimes, more than one answer is possible.

EXAMPLE:   I don't eat  __*much (a lot of)*__  sugar.

1. Sam eats _____ sugar.
2. Do you eat _____ potato chips?
3. How _____ eggs do you eat a week?
4. How _____ milk do you drink?
5. We don't buy _____ cakes.

6. Do they drink _____ water?
7. The dog eats _____ ground beef.
8. Does Lien eat _____ apples?
9. I eat _____ pancakes.
10. We don't need _____ food.

**B**  Rewrite each sentence using *a few* or *a little.*

EXAMPLE:   The children want milk.     ___*The children want a little milk.*___

1. I eat apples every week. _____
2. He always buys ham. _____
3. Irina has sugar in her coffee. _____
4. Do you need eggs? _____
5. Sometimes we order desserts. _____
6. Marie and Jean are having cookies. _____
7. Do you want soup for lunch? _____
8. Dimitri needs butter for his toast. _____
9. We often eat pancakes for breakfast. _____
10. I'm hungry. I want spaghetti. _____

*A lot of, many, much, a few, a little*

## CHALLENGE 4 ► Count/non-count nouns with units of measure

| Container | Measurement | Unit |
|---|---|---|
| carton(s) of ice cream | quart(s) of orange juice | loaf (loaves) of bread |
| bottle(s) of oil | gallon(s) of milk | piece(s) of cake |
| jar(s) of pickles | pound(s) of ham | |
| box(es) of cereal | | |
| bag(s) of flour | | |
| can(s) of soup | | |

**A**  **Circle the letter of the most appropriate container, measurement, or unit.**

EXAMPLE:   Rosa is buying a ___ of rice.      a. gallon        b. pound

1.  I need two ___ of bread.                  a. loaves        b. quarts
2.  They have many ___ of cereal in this aisle.   a. boxes      b. pieces
3.  She's buying four ___ of soup.            a. bottles       b. cans
4.  Tan needs a ___ of ground beef.           a. pound         b. box
5.  Mario is buying a ___ of vanilla ice cream.   a. loaf       b. carton
6.  Do you want a ___ of cheesecake?          a. piece         b. jar
7.  The dog eats two ___ of meat a week.      a. gallons       b. pounds
8.  We are buying one ___ of flour.           a. bag           b. cans
9.  The restaurant needs five ___ of oil.     a. loaves        b. bottles
10. They are buying two ___ of pickles.       a. gallons       b. jars

**B**  **Complete the shopping list with an appropriate container, measurement, or unit.**

*Shopping List*

| | | |
|---|---|---|
| five | **pounds** | of potatoes |
| one | | of jelly |
| two | | of bread |
| one | | of orange juice |
| a | | of vanilla ice cream |
| four | | of tomato soup |
| one | | of oil |
| two | | of chocolate cake mix |
| three | | of ground beef |
| two | | of milk |
| two | | of sugar |

# Food and Nutrition

## CHALLENGE 5 ▶ *There is, there are*

| there is, there are | |
|---|---|
| SINGULAR | **There is (There's)** a good Vietnamese restaurant in Portland.<br>**There is (There's)** one bottle of soda for lunch. |
| PLURAL | **There are** carrots in aisle four.<br>**There are** three pieces of cake. |
| QUESTIONS | **Is there** a dairy section in this supermarket?<br>**Are there** many Chinese restaurants in Los Angeles? |

- Use **there** to show or ask about place or position.

**A** Complete the sentences with *there is* or *there are*.

EXAMPLE: _____*There is*_____ a new supermarket in Newtown.

1. _____ six aisles in the supermarket.
2. _____ a checkout near the exit.
3. _____ many beverages in aisle two.
4. _____ a good bakery section.
5. _____ tomatoes, potatoes, and carrots in the produce section.
6. _____ cake mixes in aisle three.
7. _____ a section for coffee and tea.
8. _____ canned goods in aisle five.
9. _____ one aisle for baking goods.
10. _____ three old supermarkets in Newtown.

**B** Write questions using *Is there* and *Are there* and the words given.

EXAMPLE: a good American restaurant    _***Is there a good American restaurant?***_____

1. ten tables in the restaurant      _____
2. a new cook                        _____
3. many people in the restaurant today  _____
4. six main courses on the menu      _____
5. many soups and salads             _____
6. a dinner salad on the menu        _____
7. hamburgers and cheeseburgers      _____
8. many different beverages          _____
9. many special desserts             _____
10. good chocolate cheesecake        _____

## CHALLENGE 6 ▶ *Some / any*

| *some / any* | | |
|---|---|---|
| | **COUNT (PLURAL)** | **NON-COUNT** |
| **AFFIRMATIVE** | I eat **some** vegetables every day. | I often eat **some** rice for dinner. |
| **NEGATIVE** | I don't eat **any** cookies. | I don't eat **any** rice. |
| **QUESTION** | Do you have **any** cookies? | Do you have **any** rice? |
| | Do you want **some** cookies? | Do you want **some** rice? |

• In questions that are requests or offers, use **some**.

### A  Complete the sentences with *some* or *any*.

EXAMPLE:   I want ___**some**___ soup for dinner.

1.  My sister wants _____ potatoes.

2.  Do you want _____ salad?

3.  Lien often eats _____ bread with her lunch.

4.  Does she eat _____ sweets?

5.  We don't eat _____ pizza.

6.  The children want _____ pancakes for breakfast.

7.  He doesn't have _____ beef today.

8.  The dog doesn't drink _____ milk.

9.  Tan is drinking _____ tea with dinner.

10.  Do you want _____ coffee?

11.  Do you have _____ oranges?

12.  We need _____ apples.

### B  Circle the correct sentence.

EXAMPLE:   Silvia needs any bread from the supermarket. / (Silvia needs some bread from the supermarket.)

1.  She needs some green beans, too. / She needs any green beans, too.

2.  She doesn't need some carrots. / She doesn't need any carrots.

3.  Augustín wants any rice. / Augustín wants some rice.

4.  He doesn't buy any onions. / He doesn't buy some onions.

5.  They need some fish for the restaurant. / They need any fish for the restaurant.

6.  Augustín buys any beverages every week. / Augustín buys some beverages every week.

7.  We don't usually buy any ice cream. / We don't usually buy some ice cream.

8.  I don't want some ice cream. / I don't want any ice cream.

9.  Do you want some ice cream now? / Do you want any ice cream now?

10.  We are buying some cans of soup. / We are buying any cans of soup.

**UNIT 3** **Food and Nutrition**

## CHALLENGE 7 ► Tag questions with simple present

| Affirmative statement | Negative tag question | Answer | |
|---|---|---|---|
| I need an egg, | **don't** I? | Yes, you **do.** | No, you **don't.** |
| You have some apples, | **don't** you? | Yes, I **do.** | No, I **don't.** |
| He wants some soup, | **doesn't** he? | Yes, he **does.** | No, he **doesn't.** |
| We need some cookies, | **don't** we? | Yes, we **do.** | No, we **don't.** |
| They like meat, | **don't** they? | Yes, they **do.** | No, they **don't.** |

- A tag question is a short question at the end of a statement.
- Use a tag question to ask if your statement is correct.

**A** Match the tag questions to the statements. Some questions are used more than once.

EXAMPLE:   We need some milk, __*b*__

1. They like bananas, _____
2. Ivan shops at the new supermarket, _____
3. The dog eats meat, _____
4. I need flour, _____
5. Anya needs a pound of tomatoes, _____
6. Rosa and Silvia have the shopping list, _____
7. You want some ice cream, _____
8. We have some lettuce, _____
9. The restaurant has some desserts, _____
10. You buy bread every day, _____

a. don't you?
b. don't we?
c. doesn't it?
d. don't they?
e. doesn't she?
f. doesn't he?
g. don't I?

**B** Add a tag question to each statement.

EXAMPLE:   The nutrition pyramid has six food groups, __*doesn't it?*__

1. You like healthy food, _____
2. Alex eats a lot of vegetables, _____
3. We need a balanced diet, _____
4. They eat a lot of beans, _____
5. You eat two servings of fruit every day, _____
6. Children need three servings of milk a day, _____
7. Marie eats good food, _____
8. I need three to five servings of vegetables a day, _____
9. Teresa likes all types of food, _____
10. The food needs a little oil, _____

## CHALLENGE 8 ▶ Tag questions with present continuous

| Affirmative statement | Negative tag question | Answer | |
|---|---|---|---|
| I am going to the store with you, | **aren't** I? | Yes, you **are.** | No, you **aren't.** |
| You are ordering a dessert, | **aren't** you? | Yes, I **am.** | No, I**'m not.** |
| She is eating dinner, | **isn't** she? | Yes, she **is.** | No, she **isn't.** |
| We are shopping today, | **aren't** we? | Yes, we **are.** | No, we **aren't.** |
| They are drinking coffee, | **aren't** they? | Yes, they **are.** | No, they **aren't.** |

• **Am I not?** is very formal. Use **aren't I?**

**A** Match the tag questions to the statements. Some questions are used more than once.

EXAMPLE:   We're ordering spaghetti, __f__

1. You are coming to the restaurant, _____
2. We are ordering pizza for everyone, _____
3. Kenji is eating lunch at 12:00, _____
4. I am eating with you today, _____
5. We are drinking water with dinner, _____
6. The children are having milk, _____
7. You are ordering a ham sandwich, _____
8. Rosa is cooking fried noodles, _____
9. The Nguyen brothers are going to dinner now, _____
10. The dog is eating its breakfast, _____

a. aren't they?
b. aren't I?
c. isn't he?
d. isn't it?
e. isn't she?
f. aren't we?
g. aren't you?

**B** Write the tag question and short answer for each sentence.

EXAMPLE:   Your mother is going to the supermarket, __*isn't she?*__   (yes) __*Yes, she is.*__

1. We are buying some ice cream, _____   (yes) _____
2. Mario and Teresa are eating dinner, _____   (yes) _____
3. They are having ham sandwiches, _____   (no) _____
4. I am having lunch with you today, _____   (yes) _____
5. You are cooking potato soup, _____   (yes) _____
6. Augustín is buying bread, _____   (no) _____
7. Rosa is working at the restaurant, _____   (yes) _____
8. I am having a salad for dinner, _____   (no) _____
9. The dog is drinking water, _____   (yes) _____
10. You are going to the new restaurant, _____   (no) _____

## CHALLENGE 1 ▶ Review: *Wh-* questions with simple present

| *Wh-* question | | | | Answer |
|---|---|---|---|---|
| Who (Whom) | do | I | **ask** about the apartment? | You ask the real estate agent. |
| What | | you | **want** to buy? | I want to buy a two-bedroom house. |
| Where | | we | **send** the application? | You send it to the landlord. |
| How | | they | **pay** for their food? | They pay with a check. |
| When | does | he | **deposit** his paycheck? | He deposits it on Monday. |
| Why | | she | **want** to move? | Because she wants a new apartment. |
| How much | | it | **cost**? | It costs $500 a month. |

- Use **whom** in formal questions that ask about the object of the verb.
- Use **because** at the beginning of informal oral answers to *why*.

### A. Write questions with the words given.

EXAMPLE:   why / you / like / the condo     ___*Why do you like the condo?*___

1. how much / the condo / cost  _____
2. who / we / talk to about the condo  _____
3. where / Gilberto / live  _____
4. why / Anya and Ivan / live in a condo  _____
5. when / you / want / to buy a house  _____
6. where / I / get a rental application form  _____
7. what / the application form / say  _____
8. how / we / find the price of the rent  _____
9. where / Irina / want to buy furniture  _____
10. what / they / need to buy  _____

### B. Write questions (Q) for the underlined answers (A).

EXAMPLE:   **Q:** ___*Where does Mario live?*___
           **A:** Mario lives <u>in Chicago</u>.

1. **Q:** _____
   **A:** I want to buy <u>a three-bedroom house</u>.

2. **Q:** _____
   **A:** The house costs <u>$200,000</u>.

3. **Q:** _____
   **A:** Kenji wants to live <u>in an apartment</u>.

4. **Q:** _____
   **A:** Marie wants to move <u>because she needs two bedrooms.</u>

5. **Q:** _____
   **A:** They ask <u>the landlord</u> about the rent.

6. **Q:** _____
   **A:** We want to live <u>in a two-bedroom condo</u>.

7. **Q:** _____
   **A:** You need to send the rent check <u>on June 1</u>.

8. **Q:** _____
   **A:** They need <u>a house with four bedrooms</u>.

## CHALLENGE 2 ▶ Review: *Wh-* questions with present continuous

| *Wh-* word | *be* | Subject | Base verb + *ing* | Answer |
|---|---|---|---|---|
| Who (Whom) | am | I | **taking** to the house? | You are taking Silvia. |
| Where | are | you | **renting** an apartment? | I am renting an apartment on Elm St. |
| What | is | he, she | **buying?** | He, she is buying a mobile home. |
| When | are | we | **moving?** | We are moving on Sunday. |
| Why | are | they | **saving** money? | Because they want to buy a house. |
| How | are | they | **paying** the rent? | They are paying with a check. |
| How much | are | they | **asking** for the condo? | They are asking for $60,000. |

• Use **whom** in formal questions that ask about the object of the verb.

**A** Complete each sentence with the words in parentheses.

EXAMPLE:   (you / buy) What __*are you buying*__?

1. (they / take) How much _____ out of their account?
2. (I / write) Who _____ a check to?
3. (Nam-young / open) Why _____ a bank account?
4. (Irina and Alexi / save) What _____ money for?
5. (we / open) Where _____ a savings account?
6. (you / write) What _____ a check for?
7. (your brother / pay) How _____ for the house?
8. (we / make) Why _____ a budget?
9. (Teresa / get) When _____ her photo ID?
10. (I / get) When _____ my checks?

**B** Read each sentence. Then ask a question using the words in parentheses.

EXAMPLE:   Kyung is making a deposit. (when)   __*When is Kyung making a deposit?*__

1. I am writing a check. (why / you) _____
2. You are getting your checks. (when) _____
3. We are opening a savings account. (where) _____
4. They are signing the check. (why) _____
5. Your brother is paying for the house. (how) _____
6. Ana is making a budget. (why) _____
7. Mario is opening a checking account. (when) _____
8. They are paying for the condo. (how much) _____
9. You are asking about the bank. (who) _____
10. Raquel is renting. (what house) _____

# UNIT 4  Housing

## CHALLENGE 3 ▶ Combining sentences with *and*

| Subject | | | Subject | |
|---|---|---|---|---|
| **The house** | <u>is</u> in a quiet neighborhood. | | **The house** | <u>has</u> a swimming pool. |
| **The house** | <u>is</u> in a quiet neighborhood | **and** | **it** | <u>has</u> a swimming pool. |
| The house is in a quiet neighborhood and it has a swimming pool. | | | | |
| **The rooms** | <u>have</u> air conditioning. | | **The rooms** | <u>are</u> in good condition. |
| **The rooms** | <u>have</u> air conditioning | **and** | **they** | <u>are</u> in good condition. |
| The rooms have air conditioning and they are in good condition. | | | | |

 **A**  Underline the two parts of each sentence.

EXAMPLE:  <u>My apartment has five rooms</u> and <u>it has a beautiful view from the balcony.</u>

1. The rent is $800 a month and the utilities are included.
2. The living room has a fireplace and the kitchen is large.
3. Nikolai and Andrea need an apartment and they are looking in the classified ads.
4. His wife wants an apartment with three bedrooms and they need a washer/dryer.
5. Our dream house is in a friendly neighborhood and it has a swimming pool.
6. Peter and I are buying a house in September and we need new furniture.

**B**  Combine the two sentences using *and.*

EXAMPLE:  I have a new friend. Kyung's name is Kyung Kim.
   *__I have a new friend and his name is Kyung Kim.__*

1. Kyung moved here from Korea last month. Kyung lives in Arcadia, Florida.
   _____

2. The teller (female) is opening a checking account for him. The teller is also opening a savings account.
   _____

3. Kyung can get his checks immediately. Kyung can write checks from the checking account.
   _____

4. Kyung uses checks to pay for food. Kyung writes the checks in the check ledger.
   _____

5. Nam-young Kim writes the check for the rent. Nam-Young also pays for the utilities.
   _____

6. Mr. and Mrs. Kim buy clothes from Sal's Clothes. Mr. and Mrs. Kim buy food from Renco Market.
   _____

7. They pay $850 a month for rent. They need $400 a month for food.
   _____

8. Their house has three bedrooms. Their house is in a quiet neighborhood.
   _____

## CHALLENGE 4 ▶ Prepositions of place

| in | | The dishes are **in** the cupboard. |
|---|---|---|
| **on** | | The bananas are **on** the kitchen counter. |
| **over** | | The picture is **over** the refrigerator. |
| **under** | | The soap is **under** the sink. |
| **between** | | The microwave is **between** the toaster and the refrigerator. |
| **in the corner** | | The box is **in the corner.** |
| **next to** | | The nightstand is **next to** the bed. |
| **in front of** | | The vacuum cleaner is **in front of** the dishwasher. |
| **in back of** | | The yard is **in back of** the house. |

### A  Circle the correct preposition for each sentence.

EXAMPLE:   There are six rooms (in) / on my apartment.

1. The kitchen is <u>on / next to</u> the living room.
2. The microwave is <u>between / over</u> the stove.
3. The washer is <u>in the corner / in front of</u>.
4. The refrigerator is <u>next to / under</u> the stove.
5. The apples are <u>in back of / in</u> the refrigerator.
6. The butter is <u>next to / in</u> the apples.
7. The sofa is <u>between / on</u> two windows.
8. The flowers are <u>in / on</u> the coffee table.
9. The book is <u>under / in</u> the armchair.
10. The TV is <u>under / in front of</u> the armchair.
11. The vacuum cleaner is <u>in / in back of</u> the sofa.
12. The door is <u>between / over</u> the sofa and the chair.

### B  Unscramble the words to tell the location of things.

EXAMPLE:   in / is / the house / a quiet neighborhood   ___*The house is in a quiet neighborhood.*___

1. Madison Street / the house / is / on   _____
2. behind / the swimming pool / is / the house   _____
3. the  yard / of / is / in / the house / front   _____
4. are / the corner / the flowers / in   _____
5. is / the garage / next / the house / to   _____
6. over / the balcony / is / the door   _____
7. in / is / the fireplace / the living room   _____
8. between / the bathroom / is / two bedrooms   _____
9. is / under / the dishwasher / the kitchen counter   _____
10. over / the kitchen counter / the cupboard / is   _____

**UNIT 4**    **Housing**

## CHALLENGE 5 ▸ Review: *Yes/no* questions with the verb *be*

| Yes/no question | Short answer | |
|---|---|---|
| **Am I** the only applicant? | Yes, you are. | No, you aren't. |
| **Are you** the landlord? | Yes, I am. | No, I'm not. |
| **Are we** friends? | Yes, we are. | No, we aren't. |
| **Are they** interesting? | Yes, they are. | No, they aren't. |
| **Is he** a real estate agent? | Yes, he is. | No, he isn't. |
| **Is she** friendly? | Yes, she is. | No, she isn't. |
| **Is it** in good condition? | Yes, it is. | No, it isn't. |

**A**   Write *yes/no* questions with the words given.

EXAMPLE:   the apartment / large     *Is the apartment large?*

1. you / happy with the neighborhood    _____

2. we / near a school    _____

3. the view from the balcony / beautiful    _____

4. the fireplace / in the living room    _____

5. I / near a shopping mall    _____

6. the bedrooms / small    _____

7. the swimming pool / nearby    _____

8. the utilities / included    _____

**B**   Choose the answer to each question. Mark the correct bubble. Fill in the bubble completely.

|  |  |  | A | B |
|---|---|---|---|---|
| EXAMPLE:   Is the house on Madison Street? | A. Yes, it are. | B. Yes, it is. | ○ | ● |
| 1. Are you the real estate agent? | A. Yes, I is. | B. Yes, I am. | ○ | ○ |
| 2. Are the rooms comfortable? | A. Yes, they are. | B. Yes, it is. | ○ | ○ |
| 3. Am I near a grocery store? | A. No, you aren't. | B. No, you isn't. | ○ | ○ |
| 4. Is the neighborhood noisy? | A. No, it is. | B. No, it isn't. | ○ | ○ |
| 5. Are we in a new neighborhood? | A. Yes, you are. | B. No, you are. | ○ | ○ |
| 6. Is the landlord friendly? | A. Yes, she is. | B. Yes, she are. | ○ | ○ |
| 7. Is the kitchen remodeled? | A. No, it aren't. | B. No, it isn't. | ○ | ○ |
| 8. Are the utilities included? | A. Yes, they are. | B. Yes, they aren't. | ○ | ○ |
| 9. Is the yard large? | A. No, they aren't. | B. No, it isn't. | ○ | ○ |
| 10. Are we the only applicants for the house? | A. No, you are. | B. No, you aren't. | ○ | ○ |

Spelling of plural nouns

## CHALLENGE 6 ▸ Spelling of plural nouns

| Word ending | Example word | Plural addition | Plural form |
|---|---|---|---|
| vowel | house<br>banana | + **s** | houses<br>bananas |
| consonant | bedroom | + **s** | bedrooms |
| **ss, sh, ch, x** | address<br>dish<br>sandwich<br>mix | + **es** | addresses<br>dishes<br>sandwiches<br>mixes |
| vowel + **y** | day | + **s** | days |
| consonant + **y** | story | **y** changes to **ies** | stories |
| vowel + **o** | stereo | + **s** | stereos |
| consonant + **o**<br>*Exceptions:* condos, photos | potato | + **es** | potatoes |
| **f** or **fe** | loaf<br>wife | **f** changes to **ves** | loaves<br>wives |

**Irregular plurals:** man → **men**, woman → **women**, child → **children**, person → **people**

**A** Write the plural form of each noun.

EXAMPLE: window __*windows*__

1. sofa _____
2. company _____
3. dress _____
4. photo _____

5. story _____
6. box _____
7. person _____
8. bookcase _____

9. mix _____
10. Monday _____
11. loaf _____
12. stereo _____

**B** Complete each sentence with the plural form of the noun given in parentheses.

EXAMPLE: (account) Kyung Kim has two _____*accounts*_____ at the bank.

1. (child) He has two _____.
2. (friend) The Kim family is living with _____.
3. (condo) They are looking at _____ for rent.
4. (house) They are also looking at _____ for rent.
5. (agency) They are filling out rental applications at three rental _____.
6. (bedroom) They want a home with three _____.
7. (stereo) The children want large bedrooms for their furniture and their _____.
8. (bathroom) The Kims want a home with two _____.
9. (dish) They need a lot of room in the kitchen for their _____.
10. (wife) They want to meet the neighbors, Mr. Brown and Mr. Sanchez, and their _____.

## CHALLENGE 7 ▶ *This, that, these, those*

|  | Near | Not near/Far |
|---|---|---|
| SINGULAR PRONOUN | **This** is a nice apartment. | **That** is an old house. |
| SINGULAR DETERMINER | **This** apartment is noisy. | **That** house has a swimming pool. |
| PLURAL PRONOUN | **These** are my new dishes. | **Those** are cheap tables. |
| PLURAL DETERMINER | **These** flowers are $6.95. | **Those** lamps are expensive. |

- Use **this, that, these,** and **those** to identify objects and people.
- The contraction for **that + is** is **that's.**
- **This, that, these,** and **those** can be used alone or with a noun following.

**A** Identify the underlined words.

|  | SINGULAR/PLURAL | NEAR/FAR |
|---|---|---|
| EXAMPLE:   These chairs cost $100. | *plural* | *near* |
| 1.  Those beds aren't expensive. | | |
| 2.  This is a new dining room set. | | |
| 3.  These are good lamps. | | |
| 4.  That VCR is $95.00. | | |
| 5.  How much are these end tables? | | |
| 6.  That's a great value. | | |
| 7.  Those are nice vases. | | |
| 8.  How much is this dresser? | | |
| 9.  That is an amazing house. | | |
| 10.  Are these your pictures? | | |

**B** Complete the sentences with *this, that, these,* or *those*. The arrow tells you if the object is near (——▶) or far (————▶).

EXAMPLE:   **This**   ad says the rent is $650 a month. ——▶

1.  What is the price of _____ bookcases? ————▶
2.  _____ is an interesting floor plan. ————▶
3.  Which house are _____ people buying? ————▶
4.  How much are _____ beds? ——▶
5.  _____'s nice furniture. ————▶
6.  _____ is a classified ad from the newspaper. ——▶
7.  _____ houses are near schools and shopping. ——▶
8.  Is _____ a friendly neighborhood? ——▶
9.  _____ very large five-bedroom house has a swimming pool. ——▶
10.  How much does _____ apartment rent for? ————▶

**Adjectives and noun modifiers**

## CHALLENGE 8 ▸ Adjectives and noun modifiers

| Adjectives | Noun modifiers |
|---|---|
| Adjectives describe nouns.<br>    I live in a **friendly** neighborhood. | A noun can sometimes describe another noun.<br>    I need a **coffee** table. |
| Adjectives come before nouns.<br>    He likes the **big** yard. | The second noun is more general than the first.<br>    A **coffee** table is a table. |
| Adjectives do not change for plural nouns.<br>    You're buying some **new** tables. | The first noun is always singular.<br>    Where are the **coffee** tables? |
| You can put two adjectives before a noun.<br>Use a comma between the adjectives.<br>    We want a **large, old** house. | You can put a number before a noun modifier. Use<br>a hyphen between the number and the modifier.<br>    You want a **two-bedroom** apartment.<br>    (Meaning: two bedrooms, not two apartments) |

**A** **Rewrite the sentences using the adjectives in parentheses.**

EXAMPLE:   I need a VCR. (new)           _*I need a new VCR.*_____

1.  The house has a garage. (separate)        _____
2.  He's buying some flowers. (expensive)     _____
3.  The balcony has a view. (beautiful)       _____
4.  These are chairs. (comfortable)           _____
5.  I live in a neighborhood. (nice / quiet)  _____
6.  The rent for the apartment is $750. (remodeled)  _____
7.  We need a dishwasher. (good / cheap)      _____
8.  What is your address? (prior)             _____
9.  She wants to rent a house. (big)          _____
10. You want some lamps. (small)              _____

**B** **Complete each sentence using the nouns given. Put them in the correct order.**

EXAMPLE:   (ledger / check) I'm looking for my _____*check ledger*_____.

1.  (account / bank) Are you opening a _____?
2.  (ATM / card) I need my _____.
3.  (ID / photo) Do you have your _____?
4.  (application / forms) Kenji needs to fill out the _____.
5.  (house / three / story) He's renting a _____.
6.  (dream / house) We are going to buy our _____.
7.  (two / car / garage) She wants a _____.
8.  (tables / coffee) Where do you want the _____?

# UNIT 5 — Our Community

## CHALLENGE 1 ▶ Prepositions to describe location

| Preposition | Example |
|---|---|
| **in** | There is a hospital **in** Thomasville. |
| **on** | It is **on** Main Street. |
| **at** | It is **at** the intersection of Main Street and Northern Avenue. |
| **near** | It is **near** my house. |
| **between** | My house is **between** South Street and Washington Street. |
| **next to** | It is **next to** the police station. |
| **on the corner (of)** | The police station is **on the corner of** South Street and Pine Street. |
| **across from** | It is **across from** the post office. |
| **on the right** | The courthouse is **on the right.** |
| **on the left** | The fire station is **on the left.** |

**A** Look at the map of Newtown. Write *yes* or *no* for each statement.

EXAMPLE: The bank is next to the fire station. **yes**

1. The pet store is next to the coffee shop. _____
2. The bank is at the intersection of Main and High. _____
3. The fire station is across from the police station. _____
4. The park is near the library. _____
5. The hospital is on the corner of High Street. _____
6. There is a courthouse in Newtown. _____
7. The library is on High Street. _____
8. The coffee shop is between the pet store and the gas station. _____
9. You are on High Street. You turn right on Main Street. The park is on the left. _____
10. You are on High Street. You turn left on Main Street. The hospital is on the right. _____

**Newtown**

**B** Using the map, complete each sentence with the name of a place.

EXAMPLE: The school is near ___*the mall*___.

1. The movie theater is on _____.
2. The bus stop is at the end of _____.
3. The bowling alley is next to _____.
4. The hardware store is near _____.
5. The hospital is between _____ and _____.
6. The pharmacy is in _____.
7. The police station is across from _____.
8. The pet store is on the corner of _____ and _____.

## CHALLENGE 2 ▶ Imperatives to give directions and instructions

| Affirmative imperative | Negative imperative |
|---|---|
| **Go** north on Main Street. | **Don't go** south on Main Street. |
| **Walk** straight ahead for two blocks. | **Don't walk** for three blocks. |
| **Turn** left on Washington Street. | **Don't turn** right on Washington Street. |
| **Fill** in this form. | **Don't fill** in that form. |
| **Complete** the form later. | **Don't complete** the form now. |

- The imperative form of verbs is used to give directions and instructions.
- The imperative uses the base form of the verb.
- The subject is **you,** but it is not included.
- The negative imperative is **do not** + base form. The contraction is **don't.**

**A** Underline the imperatives in the following paragraph. The first one is done for you.

Here are the directions to get to my new apartment from the bank. Go north on Emerson Street. Walk straight ahead for two blocks. There is a pharmacy on the left. Turn left on Michigan Avenue. Go two blocks. At the intersection of Michigan Avenue and Lincoln Street, turn right. Don't turn left; that's the way to my old apartment. My new apartment is at the end of Lincoln Street, on the left. Walk up the stairs. Find apartment #3.

**B** If the sentence is affirmative, make it negative. If it is negative, make it affirmative.

EXAMPLES: Complete the envelope now.    _Don't complete the envelope now._

           Don't turn right on Oak Street.    _Turn right on Oak Street._

1. Go to the post office today. _____

2. Write your address on the form. _____

3. Don't send the package economy class. _____

4. Don't buy insurance for the package. _____

5. Fill in all the customs forms now. _____

6. Walk from the post office to the pharmacy. _____

7. Don't turn left at the corner. _____

8. Turn right at the next intersection. _____

9. Don't go west on Broadway. _____

10. Stop at the corner of Main and Robinson. _____

## CHALLENGE 3 ▶ Review: Simple present and frequency words

| be | Other verbs |
|---|---|
| I **am rarely** early for work. | I **always go** outside for lunch. |
| You **are sometimes** in a hurry. | You **sometimes stay** at the library for two hours. |
| He, She, It **is always** happy. | He, She, It **rarely eats** in the morning. |
| We **are often** at the bowling alley. | We **usually walk** to the mall. |
| They **are never** friendly. | They **never visit** their friends on Sunday. |

- Frequency word:     **never    rarely    sometimes    often    always**
  Frequency:              0% ◀━━━━━━━━━━━━━━━━━━▶ 100%
- With the verb **be,** frequency words come after the verb form.
- With other verbs, frequency words come before the verb form.

 **A**   Insert each frequency word in the correct place.

EXAMPLE:   The weather is ^*usually* warm. (usually)

1. The bus circles the city in exactly one hour. (always)

2. I work at the computer store on Monday. (often)

3. You are in a hurry in the morning. (usually)

4. We eat lunch at the restaurant on the corner. (rarely)

5. The bowling alley is busy. (always)

6. They eat lunch in the park. (sometimes)

7. The bus stops at the corner of Main. (never)

8. Marie is at the mall on Saturday. (often)

**B**   Complete each sentence with the verb and the frequency word given.

EXAMPLE:   (be / often) Teresa _____*is often*_____ in a hurry.

1. (eat / usually) She _____ in a fast food restaurant.

2. (go / often) Teresa and her husband, Mario, _____ to the museum on Saturday.

3. (be / always) Mario _____ happy to go to the art gallery with Teresa.

4. (visit / often) I _____ Teresa on Friday night.

5. (go / sometimes) We _____ to the movie theater.

6. (be / rarely) We _____ in a hurry to go home.

7. (go / usually) Do you _____ to the movies on the weekend?

8. (be / sometimes) On Saturday, I _____ at the mall.

9. (come / rarely) My husband _____ with me.

10. (be / always) We _____ tired on Sunday.

**UNIT 5** **Our Community**

## CHALLENGE 4 ▶ Review: Present continuous

| Subject | *be* | Base verb + *ing* | Example |
|---------|------|-------------------|---------|
| I | **am** | **sending** | I **am sending** you a package. |
| You | **are** | **buying** | You **are buying** a gift. |
| He, She, It | **is** | **walking** | He, She, It **is walking** straight ahead. |
| We | **are** | **mailing** | We **are mailing** a letter. |
| They | **are** | **visiting** | They **are visiting** their aunt. |

• You can make a contraction with the subject and a form of **be**.
   **I'm** going to the post office.          **Marie's** going to the bus station.

• To form the negative, put **not** after the form of **be**.
   **I'm not** buying envelopes.   Raquel**'s not** walking to the store.   Anya **isn't** going out tonight.

**A**  **Circle the correct present continuous verb in each sentence.**

EXAMPLE:   I going / (am going) to the dentist.

1.  You <u>are walking</u> / <u>is walking</u> to the bus station.
2.  Marie <u>is working</u> / <u>are working</u> at the hospital today.
3.  She <u>are going</u> / <u>is going</u> to the library tonight.
4.  I <u>am turning</u> / <u>turning</u> left on Oak Street.
5.  We <u>are taking</u> / <u>am taking</u> the train to Florida.
6.  Anya and Ivan <u>is staying</u> / <u>are staying</u> home.
7.  They <u>are going</u> / <u>going</u> out tomorrow.
8.  Mario <u>visiting</u> / <u>is visiting</u> his mother today.
9.  Teresa <u>is working</u> / <u>are working</u>.
10. You <u>is buying</u> / <u>are buying</u> a postcard.

**B**  **Make the following present continuous statements negative.**

EXAMPLE:   I'm writing a letter.          *I'm not writing a letter.*

1.  I'm staying with Marie for two days.          _____
2.  We're going to the post office this morning.   _____
3.  Marie's sending a package to her mother.       _____
4.  I'm mailing pictures to my cousin.             _____
5.  Marie and Jean are talking on the phone.       _____
6.  Jean is visiting a friend at the hospital.     _____
7.  I'm waiting for them to finish.                _____
8.  At ten, we're going shopping at the mall.      _____
9.  We're having lunch at a Mexican restaurant.    _____
10. You're eating lunch with us.                   _____

## CHALLENGE 5 ▶ Review: Simple present and present continuous

| Simple present | Present continuous |
|---|---|
| Marie **lives** in Palm City. | Marie **is living** in an apartment at the moment. |
| She **works** at the hospital. | Today she**'s working** from nine to five. |
| She often **writes** letters to Raquel. | She**'s writing** a letter now. |
| She **goes** to the post office every week. | She**'s going** to the coffee shop right now. |

- Use the simple present to talk about a general truth or habitual activity.
  Use the simple present with **always, often, usually, never, sometimes, every day/month/season.**
- Use the present continuous for an action in progress.
  Use the present continuous with **now, right now, at the (this) moment, today.**

**A** Choose the simple present or the present continuous. Mark the correct bubble. Fill in the bubble completely.

|  |  |  |  |  | A | B |
|---|---|---|---|---|---|---|
| EXAMPLE: | You never ___ to the hardware store. | A. are going | B. go | | ○ | ● |
| 1. | Marie ___ a new job at the hospital. | A. is having | B. has | | ○ | ○ |
| 2. | Today she ___ in the morning. | A. is working | B. works | | ○ | ○ |
| 3. | Michel sometimes ___ Marie. | A. visits | B. is visiting | | ○ | ○ |
| 4. | They always ___ to the museum. | A. are going | B. go | | ○ | ○ |
| 5. | I ___ in a condominium at the moment. | A. live | B. am living | | ○ | ○ |
| 6. | My husband and I ___ to the supermarket every day. | A. are going | B. go | | ○ | ○ |
| 7. | You usually ___ lunch at Taco Town. | A. have | B. are having | | ○ | ○ |
| 8. | Right now you ___ in the park. | A. are eating | B. eat | | ○ | ○ |

**B** Complete each sentence with the correct form of the simple present or the present continuous.

EXAMPLE:  (go) I _____*am going*_____ to the dentist today.

1. (walk) I often _____ to the dentist.
2. (take) Today I _____ the bus.
3. (go) My sister usually _____ with me.
4. (wait) At the moment, we _____ at the bus stop on Main Street.
5. (stop) The bus always _____ at the corner of Main and Washington.
6. (take) Anya and Ivan often _____ the bus, too.
7. (go) They _____ to the travel agency right now.
8. (visit) Every summer, they _____ their family in Russia.
9. (wait) You sometimes _____ for the bus at the stop on High Street.
10. (read) At the moment, you _____ the newspaper at the bus stop.

UNIT
5    Our Community

## CHALLENGE 6 ▶ Prepositions of time

| Preposition | Example |
|---|---|
| **on:** days<br>dates | I am going to the bank **on** Saturday.<br>City Hall is not open **on** July 4. |
| **at:** a specific time<br>*night* | I am going to the dentist **at** 3:00 P.M.<br>We go to the library **at** night. |
| **in:** amount of time<br>months<br>seasons<br>*the morning/afternoon/evening* | He's going to Japan **in** two hours.<br>He always visits his sister **in** August.<br>The weather is very warm **in** the summer.<br>We go to the bowling alley **in** the afternoon. |

**A**  **Circle the correct preposition for each sentence.**

EXAMPLE:   Stefan always visits Kenji at / (in) the summer.

1. He usually comes in / on August.

2. This year, he is coming in / on July 14.

3. His bus arrives at / in 10:00 A.M.

4. It arrives in / at night.

5. Kenji and Stefan are going to the museum in / on Sunday.

6. They're going in / at the afternoon.

7. They're going to the theater in / at the evening.

8. The show is at / on 8:30 P.M.

9. In / On two hours, they're going to the mall.

10. Stefan is going home on / at July 20.

11. Kenji wants to visit Stefan in / at May.

12. He likes to travel on / in the spring.

**B**  **Complete each sentence with the correct preposition.**

EXAMPLE:   Palm City is a wonderful place to visit ___*in*___ the summer.

1. The temperature is usually 80 degrees Fahrenheit _____ the afternoon.

2. _____ night, it is often about 70 degrees.

3. It was 85 degrees _____ July 30.

4. People in Palm City sometimes eat their lunch in the park _____ 12:00 P.M.

5. They also like to walk in the park _____ the evening.

6. The children always play in the playgrounds _____ June, July, and August.

7. You usually see them in the playgrounds _____ Friday and Saturday.

8. Palm City is also a nice place to visit _____ the winter.

9. Most of the time, the weather is warm _____ January.

10. The temperature is usually about 65 degrees _____ 8:00 A.M.

# UNIT 5 — Our Community

## CHALLENGE 7 ▶ Using *there* + *be*

| Affirmative statement | Negative statement |
|---|---|
| **There is (There's)** a bank in Middleton. | **There isn't** a train station in Middleton. |
| **There are** two pharmacies in Middleton. | **There aren't** any movie theaters. |
| **Yes/no question** | **Short answer** |
| **Is there** a bowling alley in Middleton? | Yes, **there is.**   No, **there isn't.** |
| **Are there** any factories in Middleton? | Yes, **there are.**   No, **there aren't.** |

• Use **any** to introduce a plural noun in a negative statement or a *yes/no* question.

**A** Look at the map of Youngstown. Complete each sentence with *There is, There isn't, There are,* or *There aren't.*

EXAMPLE: _____**There's**_____ a coffee shop in Youngstown.

1. _____ two gas stations.
2. _____ any pharmacies.
3. _____ a hardware store.
4. _____ a police station.
5. _____ any bowling alleys.
6. _____ a big park.
7. _____ two banks.
8. _____ a museum.

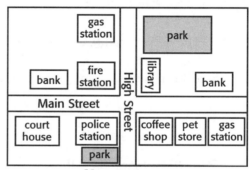

**Youngstown**

**B** Answer the questions about Youngstown according to the map above.

EXAMPLE:  Is there a coffee shop in Youngstown?    _____**Yes, there is.**_____

1. Is there a bank next to the pet store? _____
2. Is there a fire station? _____
3. Are there any banks? _____
4. Is there a computer store near the library? _____
5. Are there any factories? _____
6. Is there a police station on the corner of Main Street? _____
7. Are there any banks on High Street? _____
8. Are there any parks? _____
9. Is there a coffee shop on Main Street? _____
10. Are there any gas stations? _____

Verbs followed by an infinitive

## CHALLENGE 8 ▶ Verbs followed by an infinitive

| Subject | Verb | Infinitive | |
|---------|------|-----------|---|
| I | **want** | **to go** | to the movie theater. |
| Marie | **needs** | **to call** | Raquel. |
| We | **love** | **to eat** | at Taco Town. |
| You | **don't like** | **to eat** | at Pizza Palace. |
| They | **are trying** | **to call** | the doctor. |

• An infinitive is **to** + the base form of a verb: **to send, to take, to be, to have.**

• An infinitive is often used after the following verbs:

    **want   need   like   love   ask   try**

**A** Circle the correct verb.

EXAMPLE:   They need (to go)/ go to the dentist.

1. Raquel is trying <u>fill / to fill</u> out the customs form.

2. She needs <u>to call / to calling</u> for information.

3. I need <u>buying / to buy</u> an envelope.

4. I want <u>to send / send</u> a letter.

5. We love <u>goes / to go</u> out to eat.

6. We don't want <u>to eats / to eat</u> at the coffee shop.

7. Marco is asking <u>going / to go</u> to the mall, too.

8. He likes <u>to shop / not to shop</u> at Sports Plus.

9. You want <u>to coming / to come</u> with me.

10. They don't need <u>go / to go</u> to work today.

**B** Unscramble the words to write sentences with infinitives.

EXAMPLE:   wants / to / Raquel / go / shopping    ***Raquel wants to go shopping.***

1. buy / a new dress / she / needs / to

2. shopping / Marie / go / loves / to / too

3. they / this / are / to / go / trying / afternoon

4. new clothes / I / buy / don't / to / need

5. the bowling alley / want / to / I / to / go

6. asking / too / my brothers / are / to / go

7. to / we / our friends / call / need

8. with us / come / want / to / they

9. the bowling alley / don't / to / you / to / like / go

10. go / like / the entertainment center / to / to / you

## CHALLENGE 1 ▶ Simple past tense of regular verbs

| Base | Past | Example |
|------|------|---------|
| **walk** | **walked** | I **walked** two miles every day last week. |
| **talk** | **talked** | You **talked** to the doctor yesterday. |
| **play** | **played** | He/She **played** soccer once a week. |
| **exercise** | **exercised** | We **exercised** on Saturday. |
| **reduce** | **reduced** | They **reduced** their blood pressure. |

- The past tense form of regular verbs is the same for all persons.
- For most verbs ending in a consonant, add **-ed: worked.**
- If the base ends in a vowel, add **-d: lived.**
- If the base ends in a vowel + **y,** do *not* change the **y: stayed.**
- For a one-syllable verb ending in *consonant + vowel + consonant,* double the final consonant and add **-ed: stopped.**

**A**   **Write the simple past tense of these verbs.**

EXAMPLE:   smoke _____ ***smoked*** _____

1. chew _____
2. continue _____
3. shop _____
4. look _____
5. like _____
6. miss _____

7. move _____
8. need _____
9. stay _____
10. exercise _____
11. want _____
12. live _____

**B**   **Complete each sentence with the simple past tense of the verb in parentheses.**

EXAMPLE:   (exercise) Last week, Alex _____ ***exercised*** _____ every day.

1. (play) He also _____ tennis on Saturday.
2. (want) His wife, Irina, _____ to play tennis on Saturday, too.
3. (visit) On Sunday, she _____ her mother, Anya.
4. (ask) The children _____ to go to the miniature golf course on Saturday afternoon.
5. (stay) They _____ until 5:00.
6. (walk) Last Saturday, I _____ five miles with my sister.
7. (need) We _____ to get some exercise.
8. (lower) My sister _____ her blood pressure by walking every day.
9. (smoke) You _____ a lot last year.
10. (stop) But you _____ last month.

## CHALLENGE 2 ▶ Simple past tense of *be* and *have*

| Base | Subject | Past | Example |
|------|---------|------|---------|
| **be** | I<br>he, she, it | **was** | I **was** a patient.<br>He, She, It **was** tired. |
| | we<br>you<br>they | **were** | We **were** nervous.<br>You **were** in the hospital.<br>They **were** at the doctor's office. |
| **have** | I<br>you<br>he, she, it<br>we<br>they | **had** | I **had** a fever.<br>You **had** a stomachache.<br>He, She, It **had** a broken leg.<br>We **had** high blood pressure.<br>They **had** an appointment at 3:00. |

**A** Circle the correct simple past verb form for each sentence.

EXAMPLE:   Last year, Luc has / (had) some health problems.

1. He was / were in the hospital a lot.

2. His wife be / was very nervous.

3. I were / was very healthy last year.

4. I had / having a good exercise plan.

5. You were / was sick last week.

6. You had / having a headache.

7. My wife and I has / had a bad day yesterday.

8. We was / were both very tired.

9. My dog had / have a broken leg last year.

10. The children was / were very sad about it.

**B** Use the words to write simple past tense sentences.

EXAMPLE:   Yesterday  I / be / tired during the day    *Yesterday I was tired during the day.*

1. I / have / a stomachache, too    _____

2. you / be / sick last week    _____

3. you / have / a cough and a fever    _____

4. this morning Ken / be / nervous    _____

5. he / have / a bad headache    _____

6. Mr. and Mrs. Ito / have / a lot of health problems    _____

7. Mr. Ito / have / a heart attack    _____

8. Mrs. Ito / be / in the hospital in June    _____

9. we / be / very healthy    _____

10. we / have / checkups in May    _____

## CHALLENGE 3 ► Simple past tense of irregular verbs

| Verbs with a spelling change in the simple past tense | | |
|---|---|---|
| break – broke | find – found | sit – sat |
| buy – bought | get – got | sleep – slept |
| come – came | go – went | take – took |
| do – did | pay – paid | understand – understood |
| drink – drank | read – read* | wake – woke |
| drive – drove | say – said** | wear – wore |
| eat – ate | see – saw | write – wrote |

\* the past tense sounds like *red*          \*\* *said* rhymes with *red*

| Verbs with no change in the simple past tense | | |
|---|---|---|
| hurt – hurt | put – put | cost – cost |

**A**   Complete each sentence with the simple past tense of the verb in parentheses.

EXAMPLE:   (break) I ___**broke**___ my arm last week.

1.  (drive) My brother _____ to the hospital.
2.  (wake) You _____ up at 7:00.
3.  (go) You _____ to the doctor at noon.
4.  (buy) Your parents _____ you some aspirin.
5.  (come) They _____ to visit you.
6.  (do) Teresa _____ some exercises.
7.  (eat) She _____ a healthy breakfast.
8.  (sleep) Dan _____ eight hours last night.
9.  (take) He _____ some vitamins.
10. (get) I _____ sick yesterday.
11. (say) My sister _____ she was sick, too.
12. (drink) We _____ a lot of orange juice.

**B**   Change each sentence from the simple present to the simple past tense.

EXAMPLE:   I wake up at 6:00 A.M.          ___*I woke up at 6:00 A.M.*_____

1.  My throat hurts.          _____
2.  You drive me to the doctor at noon.          _____
3.  The doctor says to take some medicine.          _____
4.  I get the medicine from the doctor.          _____
5.  You read the directions.          _____
6.  I drink two teaspoons of the syrup.          _____
7.  I sleep for ten hours.          _____
8.  We eat a good breakfast.          _____
9.  My friends come to see me.          _____
10. They buy me some flowers.          _____

## CHALLENGE 4 ▸ Questions with *was* and *were*

| *Yes/no* question | Short answer | |
|---|---|---|
| **Were** you tired last night? | Yes, I **was**. | No, I **wasn't**. |
| **Was** Kim late for work? | Yes, he **was**. | No, he **wasn't**. |
| **Were** they at the pharmacy? | Yes, they **were**. | No, they **weren't**. |
| *Wh-* question | Answer | |
| Where **were** you yesterday? | I **was** in the park. | |
| How **was** she last night? | She **was** very sick. | |
| When **were** we late? | We **were** late on Tuesday. | |

**A** Read each statement. First write a *yes/no* question with the words in parentheses. Then write a short answer.

EXAMPLE:   I was sick yesterday. (you)   <u>Were you sick yesterday?</u>   (no) <u>No, I wasn't.</u>

1. You were at the hospital. (Tan)   _____ (yes) _____
2. They were nervous. (we)   _____ (no) _____
3. Anya was tired all the time. (you)   _____ (yes) _____
4. I was unconscious. (Maria)   _____ (no) _____
5. We were late for the appointment. (I)   _____ (yes) _____
6. Irina was very healthy. (you)   _____ (yes) _____
7. Lien was with the doctor. (the boys)   _____ (yes) _____
8. You were at the dentist. (they)   _____ (no) _____

**B** Read each statement. Then write a *wh-* question with the word in parentheses.

EXAMPLE:   I was nervous yesterday. (why)   <u>Why was I nervous yesterday?</u>

1. The children were in the park. (when)   _____
2. Sara was an optometrist. (where)   _____
3. We were healthy all the time. (why)   _____
4. Mr. Nakamura was a dentist. (when)   _____
5. She was a famous doctor. (who)   _____
6. You were in the hospital. (why)   _____
7. The dog was sick. (when)   _____
8. I was late for the exercise class. (why)   _____
9. Mario was a new patient. (where)   _____
10. It was at the pharmacy. (what)   _____

**UNIT 6** **Health**

## CHALLENGE 5 ► Negative form of simple past tense verbs

| Affirmative statement | Negative statement |
|---|---|
| I **played** soccer last weekend. | Sonia **didn't play** soccer last weekend. |
| You **slept** late yesterday. | We **didn't sleep** late yesterday. |
| Marco **was** sick last week. | Trinh **wasn't** sick last week. |
| They **were** very tired. | We **weren't** very tired. |

• To form negative statements in the past with **be**, use **was not (wasn't)** and **were not (weren't)**.

• For all other verbs, regular or irregular, use **did not (didn't)** + the base form.

**A** Rewrite each sentence in the negative using the words in parentheses. Use a contraction.

EXAMPLE:   Yesterday was a bad day. (Monday)   ___*Monday wasn't a bad day.*___

1.  I woke up late. (you)   _____
2.  Rosa was sick. (Amy)   _____
3.  Toshio had a backache. (Andre)   _____
4.  You had a toothache. (I)   _____
5.  Lara broke her arm. (my aunt)   _____
6.  The boy had a fever. (the girl)   _____
7.  We were late for work. (the doctors)   _____
8.  Ali and Ana needed to see the doctor. (we)   _____
9.  My head hurt. (my feet)   _____
10. I went to the hospital. (Ali and Ana)   _____

**B** Answer each question with a negative statement.

EXAMPLE:   Did you go to the dentist yesterday?   ___*No, I didn't go to the dentist yesterday.*___

1.  Did Marie have a cold?   _____
2.  Was she at the doctor's office?   _____
3.  Did you play soccer yesterday?   _____
4.  Did you hurt your shoulder?   _____
5.  Were the girls in school last week?   _____
6.  Did they have the flu?   _____
7.  Did Kenji drive to the hospital?   _____
8.  Did he go with the ambulance?   _____
9.  Did I break my nose?   _____
10. Did we lower our blood pressure?   _____

**Questions with simple past tense**

## CHALLENGE 6 ▶ Questions with simple past tense

| Yes/no question | Short answer | |
|---|---|---|
| **Did** you **exercise** yesterday? | Yes, I **did.** | No, I **didn't.** |
| **Did** he **have** an earache? | Yes, he **did.** | No, he **didn't.** |
| **Did** we **buy** any aspirin? | Yes, we **did.** | No, we **didn't.** |

• For *yes/no* questions in the simple past tense (regular or irregular verbs), use **did** + the base form.

| Wh- question | Answer |
|---|---|
| Where **did** you **play** soccer yesterday? | I played soccer in the park. |
| How **did** she **get** to the doctor's office? | She took the bus. |
| When **did** they **have** an appointment? | They had an appointment at 3:00. |

• For *wh-* questions in the simple past tense, use **did** + the base form.

**A**  Read each answer. Write a *yes/no* question with the words in parentheses and a short negative answer.

EXAMPLE:   **Q:** (she / fever)  ___*Did she have a fever?*_____

   **A:** No, __*she didn't*_____. She had a cold.

1.  **Q:** (you / headache) _____
   **A:** No, _____. I had a stomachache.

2.  **Q:** (Rosa / Monday) _____
   **A:** No, _____. Rosa exercised on Friday.

3.  **Q:** (you / dentist) _____
   **A:** No, _____. I went to the doctor.

4.  **Q:** (they / warnings) _____
   **A:** No, _____. They read the directions.

5.  **Q:** (you / orange juice) _____
   **A:** No, _____. We drank a lot of water.

6.  **Q:** (the cat / its foot) _____
   **A:** No, _____. The cat broke its leg.

**B**  Unscramble the words to write *wh-* questions in the simple past tense.

EXAMPLE:   last year / did / when / see / the doctor / we   __*When did we see the doctor last year?*_____

1.  did / what / the doctor / say   _____
2.  pay / did / you / how   _____
3.  buy / Marina / where / did / the medicine   _____
4.  she / did / who / the pills / for / buy   _____
5.  smoking / when / your parents / did / stop   _____
6.  every / did / why / exercise / day / they   _____

## CHALLENGE 7 ▸ *Should*

| Example | Use |
|---|---|
| You **should** take two aspirin. | To give advice |
| He **should not** chew the tablets. | To give a warning |

- **Should** never takes an **-s**: He **should** exercise more. (*not:* He should$ exercise more.)
- Use the verb base form after **should** and **should not**.
- The contraction for **should not** is **shouldn't**.

**A** Read the problems. Give advice, using the words in parentheses.

EXAMPLE: I need some aspirin. (go to the drugstore) ___*You should go to the drugstore.*___

1. We are very tired. (sleep eight hours tonight) _____

2. Ricardo has a cough. (take some cough syrup) _____

3. I broke my arm. (go to the hospital) _____

4. You have a fever. (go to bed) _____

5. Luisa has a headache. (take some aspirin) _____

6. Those men smoke too much. (stop smoking) _____

7. My eyes hurt. (go to the optometrist) _____

8. Mrs. Ramos has high blood pressure.
   (lower her blood pressure)

**B** Complete the sentences with *should* or *shouldn't*.

EXAMPLE: You _____*shouldn't*_____ play soccer today. (no)

1. I _____ stop smoking. (yes)

2. Carla _____ eat fatty foods. (no)

3. You _____ take aspirin if you have the chicken pox. (no)

4. The children _____ have a checkup every year. (yes)

5. We _____ talk on the phone when we drive. (no)

6. Ivan _____ take his medicine three times a day. (yes)

7. You _____ make an appointment with the doctor. (yes)

8. They _____ be nervous all the time. (no)

9. I _____ take some cough syrup for my cough. (yes)

10. We _____ drink too much coffee. (no)

# UNIT 6 Health

## CHALLENGE 8 ▶ Questions with *should*

| Yes/no question | Short answer | |
|---|---|---|
| **Should** I **exercise** every day? | Yes, you **should.** | No, you **shouldn't.** |
| **Should** he **have** a check-up? | Yes, he **should.** | No, he **shouldn't.** |
| **Should** we **buy** some vitamins? | Yes, we **should.** | No, we **shouldn't.** |
| Wh- question | Answer | |
| Who **should** I **ask** about the medicine? | You **should** ask the doctor. | |
| Where **should** she **buy** the cough syrup? | She **should** buy the cough syrup at the pharmacy. | |
| Why **should** we **take** the pills? | Because we have a cough and a fever. | |

• For *yes/no* questions and *wh-* questions, use **should** + the base form.

**A** Unscramble the words to write *yes/no* questions with *should.*

EXAMPLE:   the / go / should / to / dentist / you       *Should you go to the dentist?*

1. coffee / should / drink / I  _____
2. three meals a day / should / eat / Eva  _____
3. reduce / should / the fever / the medicine  _____
4. a checkup / should / have / Mario  _____
5. you / chew / the tablets / should  _____
6. an appointment / make / they / should  _____
7. should / an ambulance / call / I  _____
8. should / smoking / stop / your parents  _____

**B** Read each statement. Then write a *wh-* question with the word in parentheses.

EXAMPLE:   You should exercise every day. (why)       *Why should I exercise every day?*

1. Your mother should lose weight. (how)  _____
2. Rosa should take her medicine. (when)  _____
3. You should run every day. (why)  _____
4. The children should play soccer. (where)  _____
5. We should visit today. (who)  _____
6. Tan and Diem should go to the dentist. (when)  _____
7. Vladimir should take aspirin. (why)  _____
8. I should eat tonight. (what)  _____
9. You should call in the morning. (who)  _____
10. We should call for an appointment. (where)  _____

# UNIT 7 | Work, Work, Work

## CHALLENGE 1 ► Simple past tense: More forms

| More regular verbs with a spelling change in the simple past tense | | |
|---|---|---|
| apply – applied | classify – classified | dry – dried |

• If the base ends in a consonant + **y**, change the **y** to **i** and add **ed.**

| More irregular verbs with a spelling change in the simple past tense | | |
|---|---|---|
| choose – chose | make – made | speak – spoke |
| keep – kept | sell – sold | spend – spent |
| know – knew | send – sent | |

| More irregular verbs with no change in the simple past tense | | |
|---|---|---|
| put – put | shut – shut | |

| REVIEW: Some irregular verbs in the simple past tense | | |
|---|---|---|
| come – came | go – went | take – took |
| do – did | have – had | understand – understood |
| get – got | see – saw | write – wrote |

 **A** Cover the words above and write the simple past tense of these verbs.

EXAMPLE: keep ___**kept**___

1. put _____
2. make _____
3. apply _____
4. do _____

5. sell _____
6. go _____
7. send _____
8. shut _____

9. write _____
10. speak _____
11. know _____
12. see _____

 **B** Change these simple present sentences to the simple past tense.

EXAMPLE: I have a new job. ___*I had a new job.*___

1. We make fax machines. _____
2. You do a lot of typing. _____
3. Mr. Lee drives a truck. _____
4. They take orders on the telephone. _____
5. We sell paper for copiers. _____
6. Youssouf speaks French at his job. _____
7. Teresa writes letters every day. _____
8. You spend a lot of time on the telephone. _____
9. I put paper in the printer in the morning. _____
10. The assistants keep the files in order. _____

Review: Negative forms of simple past tense verbs

## CHALLENGE 2 ▶ Review: Negative forms of simple past tense verbs

| Negative forms of regular and irregular verbs (except *be*) | |
| --- | --- |
| I **didn't work** in the evenings. | We **didn't have** a paid vacation. |
| Dalva **didn't know** how to type. | You **didn't turn off** the computer. |

• For all forms of regular and irregular verbs (except **be**), use **did not (didn't)** + base.

| Negative forms of *be* | |
| --- | --- |
| I **wasn't** at work today. | We **weren't** happy. |
| He, She, It **wasn't** friendly. | You **weren't** in the hospital. |
| | They **weren't** at the front desk. |

• For the verb **be**, use **was not (wasn't)** and **were not (weren't)**.

**A**  Choose the negative form to complete each sentence in the simple past tense. Mark the correct bubble. Fill in the bubble completely.

|  | | | | A | B |
| --- | --- | --- | --- | --- | --- |
| EXAMPLE: They ___ the phone. | A. didn't answered | B. didn't answer | | ○ | ● |
| 1. I ___ an administrative assistant. | A. weren't | B. wasn't | | ○ | ○ |
| 2. Last year, Marie ___ health insurance. | A. didn't have | B. doesn't have | | ○ | ○ |
| 3. The resumes ___ on my desk. | A. weren't | B. wasn't | | ○ | ○ |
| 4. Geraldo ___ as a gardener. | A. not work | B. didn't work | | ○ | ○ |
| 5. Marie ___ French at her old job. | A. didn't speak | B. didn't spoke | | ○ | ○ |
| 6. You ___ about my new job. | A. didn't ask | B. didn't asked | | ○ | ○ |
| 7. We ___ the job ads yesterday. | A. don't read | B. didn't read | | ○ | ○ |
| 8. I ___ out the job application. | A. didn't fill | B. didn't fills | | ○ | ○ |

**B**  Complete the sentences with the negative form of the underlined verb.

EXAMPLE:  Dalva <u>worked</u> at a hotel. She _____*didn't work*_____ at a hospital.

1. She <u>checked</u> the reservations. She _____ the job applications.

2. I <u>typed</u> letters all day. I _____ e-mails.

3. I <u>was</u> available for work on Saturday. I _____ available for work on Sunday.

4. You <u>were</u> interested in a full-time job. You _____ interested in a part-time job.

5. You <u>knew</u> how to use the fax machine. You _____ how to use the shredder.

6. We <u>were</u> at the copier. We _____ at the printer.

7. They <u>offered</u> free training. They _____ health insurance.

8. Youssouf <u>kept</u> all the files. He _____ all the software programs.

9. He <u>was</u> at the office all day. He _____ at home.

10. My sister <u>applied</u> for a job as a legal assistant. She _____ for a job as a clerk.

## CHALLENGE 3 ▶ Tag questions with simple past

| Affirmative statement | Negative tag question | Answer | |
|---|---|---|---|
| I got the job, | **didn't** I? | Yes, you **did.** | No, you **didn't.** |
| You had an interview, | **didn't** you? | Yes, I **did.** | No, I **didn't.** |
| He filed the letters, | **didn't** he? | Yes, he **did.** | No, he **didn't.** |
| She was late today, | **wasn't** she? | Yes, she **was.** | No, she **wasn't.** |
| They were programmers, | **weren't** they? | Yes, they **were.** | No, they **weren't.** |

- In the simple past for most verbs, tag questions use **did** + **not** (**didn't**) + subject pronoun.
- In the simple past for **be**, tag questions use **was** + subject pronoun (**I, he, she it**) or **were** + subject pronoun (**we, you, they**).

**A** Match the tag questions to the statements. Some questions are used more than once.

EXAMPLE:  We got the job application, __*b*__

1. They filled out the application, _____
2. Gilberto started his new job, _____
3. The job was in the classified ads, _____
4. I worked well with the team, _____
5. Sara was a sales assistant, _____
6. They were police officers, _____
7. You had a positive attitude, _____
8. I understood the job, _____
9. We followed instructions, _____
10. You were on time for the interview, _____

a. didn't you?
b. didn't we?
c. wasn't it?
d. didn't they?
e. wasn't she?
f. didn't he?
g. didn't I?
h. weren't you?
i. weren't they?

**B** Add a tag question to each statement. Then answer the question.

EXAMPLE:  You applied for a part-time job, __*didn't you?*__          (yes) __*Yes, I did.*__

1. You got the job, _____          (no) _____
2. Dalva was an administrative assistant, _____          (yes) _____
3. She talked to the hotel guests, _____          (no) _____
4. They had some job openings, _____          (yes) _____
5. The jobs were full-time positions, _____          (no) _____
6. I wrote my social security number, _____          (yes) _____
7. I was the only applicant, _____          (no) _____
8. Youssouf worked at Datamix Computers, _____          (yes) _____
9. He was a programmer in 1996, _____          (no) _____
10. We learned the job quickly, _____          (yes) _____

Using *can* to describe ability

## CHALLENGE 4 ▶ Using *can* to describe ability

|  | Subject | *can* | *Base* | Example |
|---|---|---|---|---|
| **AFFIRMATIVE** | I | **can** | type | I **can** type 60 words a minute. |
|  | he, she, it | **can** | use | He, She **can** use a computer. |
|  | we | **can** | fix | We **can** fix things around the house. |
| **NEGATIVE** | you | **cannot** | speak | You **cannot** speak Spanish. |
|  | they | **can't** | turn | They **can't** turn on the copier. |

• The negative of **can** is **cannot**. The contraction is **can't**.

**A**   **Say what these people *can* and *can't* do.**

EXAMPLE:   Kenji _____**can**_____ use a computer. (yes)

1.  I _____ type quickly. (no)

2.  Marie _____ speak Japanese. (no)

3.  Anya and Ivan _____ use e-mail. (yes)

4.  You _____ put the paper in the printer. (no)

5.  We _____ work well together. (yes)

6.  I _____ turn on the fax machine. (no)

7.  They _____ understand Chinese. (yes)

8.  We _____ drive a car. (yes)

9.  Sam _____ speak English well. (no)

10.  Gilberto _____ prepare food. (yes)

11.  I _____ cook well. (no)

12.  You _____ teach English. (yes)

**B**   **Unscramble the words to write sentences about what people *can* and *cannot* do.**

EXAMPLE:   speak / cannot / Russian / I        ___*I cannot speak Russian.*___

1.  can / soccer / you / play        _____

2.  Sara / the piano / can't / play        _____

3.  draw / well / cannot / we        _____

4.  can / the house / things / around / Ivan / fix        _____

5.  the computer / Dalva / use / can        _____

6.  a truck / you / drive / can't        _____

7.  the children / swim / can        _____

8.  Spanish / teach / cannot / I        _____

9.  cook / food / Mexican / Mario / can        _____

10.  can't / Chinese / we / understand        _____

UNIT
7    **Work, Work, Work**

## CHALLENGE 5 ► Other uses of *can*

| Example | Explanation |
|---|---|
| You **can** get a part-time job. | Possibility |
| He **cannot** answer the phone now. | No possibility |
| We **can** go home at 4:00 P.M. | Permission |
| They **can't** use that computer today. | No permission |

 **Label the purpose of *can* in each sentence. Write *ability, possibility, no possibility, permission*, or *no permission*.**

EXAMPLE:   I can send my resume tomorrow.          *possibility*

1.  You can use my computer if you need it.          _____

2.  Irina can't work today because she has a class.          _____

3.  We can understand Portuguese.          _____

4.  Mr. Lee can't make a delivery today.          _____

5.  They cannot work in my office.          _____

6.  You can speak many languages.          _____

7.  We can offer training and good benefits.          _____

8.  I can work full-time or part-time.          _____

9.  Mario can use my car today.          _____

10.  You cannot use my telephone.          _____

**B** **Use the words to write sentences with *can* and *can't*.**

EXAMPLE:   you / not / go to work tomorrow          *You can't go to work tomorrow.*

1.  I / fix copiers and fax machines          _____

2.  Michel / not / drive a truck          _____

3.  we / find a job in the local newspaper          _____

4.  they / get an application form today          _____

5.  you / not / wear shorts to work          _____

6.  Tina / use my telephone now          _____

7.  we / not use the Internet at work          _____

8.  I / start the new job today          _____

9.  Yuri and Luis / not / follow instructions          _____

10.  you / work well with the team          _____

## UNIT 7 | Work, Work, Work

### CHALLENGE 6 ▶ Questions with *can*

| Yes/no question | Short answer |
|---|---|
| **Can** you type 45 words per minute? | Yes, I **can**.     No, I **can't**. |
| **Can't** he work today? | Yes, he **can**.     No, he **can't**. |
| Wh- question | Answer |
| Where **can** I find a part-time job? | You **can** find a part-time job in the newspaper. |
| How many words per minute **can** you type? | I **can** type 60 words per minute. |
| When **can** they send the references? | They **can** send the references on Monday. |
| Why **can't** she use your car? | She **can't** use my car because I need it today. |

**A** Write *yes/no* questions to ask what these people *can* and *can't* do.

EXAMPLE:   Diem / drive a car          _**Can Diem drive a car?**_

1. Anya and Ivan / work on Saturday     _____

2. you / send me a resume     _____

3. I / file those letters     _____

4. Teresa / not / speak French     _____

5. we / talk about the job     _____

6. they / not / get job training     _____

7. Don / give me his social security number     _____

8. I / not / use your computer     _____

**B** Write *wh-* questions (Q) with *can/can't* for the underlined answers (A).

EXAMPLE:   Q: _**Who can use a computer?**_
              A: <u>Mario</u> can use a computer.

1. Q: _____
   A: I can work <u>Monday through Friday</u>.

2. Q: _____
   A: She can't drive <u>because she didn't learn how</u>.

3. Q: _____
   A: We can check <u>reservations and e-mails</u>.

4. Q: _____
   A: You can't wear <u>shorts and T-shirts</u> to work.

5. Q: _____
   A: They can send the references <u>next week</u>.

6. Q: _____
   A: <u>Ricardo</u> can speak Spanish and English.

7. Q: _____
   A: You can use the phone <u>in my office</u>.

8. Q: _____
   A: I can't work today <u>because I'm sick</u>.

**UNIT 7** **Work, Work, Work**

## CHALLENGE 7 ► Tag questions with *can*

| | Statement | Tag question | Answer | |
|---|---|---|---|---|
| **AFFIRMATIVE** | I can work part-time, | **can't** I? | Yes, you **can.** | No, you **can't.** |
| | You can type, | **can't** you? | Yes, I **can.** | No, I **can't.** |
| | He can drive a truck, | **can't** he? | Yes, he **can.** | No, he **can't.** |
| **NEGATIVE** | She can't work today, | **can** she? | Yes, she **can.** | No, she **can't.** |
| | They can't cook, | **can** they? | Yes, they **can.** | No, they **can't.** |

- An affirmative statement uses a negative tag.
- A negative statement uses an affirmative tag.

**A** **Circle the correct tag question for each statement.**

EXAMPLE:   You can come to work today, (can't you) / can you?

1. You can't work on Saturday, <u>can't you / can you</u>?
2. Dalva can type, <u>can she / can't she</u>?
3. She can work in the evenings, <u>can't she / doesn't she</u>?
4. They can't use a computer, <u>can they / do they</u>?
5. They can learn quickly, <u>don't they / can't they</u>?
6. I can get paid hourly, <u>can't I / aren't I</u>?
7. I can't work part-time, <u>can I / can't I</u>?
8. Youssouf can't speak Spanish, <u>can't he / can he</u>?
9. He can change his job, <u>doesn't he / can't he</u>?
10. We can fill out a job application, <u>can't we / can we</u>?

**B** **Add a tag question to each statement. Then answer the question.**

EXAMPLE:   You can work full-time, ___*can't you?*___   (yes) ___*Yes, I can.*___

1. You can't work on weekends, _____ (yes) _____
2. We can wear shorts to work, _____ (no) _____
3. We can't use the shredder, _____ (yes) _____
4. They can get job training, _____ (yes) _____
5. They can't get health insurance, _____ (no) _____
6. I can't get free rent, _____ (no) _____
7. I can get a paid vacation, _____ (yes) _____
8. Abdul can get a pension, _____ (no) _____
9. He can also get health insurance, _____ (yes) _____
10. You can offer him the job, _____ (yes) _____

## CHALLENGE 8 ▶ Review: Imperatives

| Affirmative imperative | Negative imperative |
|---|---|
| **Write** your name on the application. | **Don't write** your age. |
| **Press** the green button. | **Don't press** the red button. |
| **Be** helpful at work. | **Don't be** late for work. |

- The imperative uses the base form of the verb.
- The subject is **you,** but it is not included.
- The negative imperative is **do not** + base form. The contraction is **don't**.
- Imperatives give warnings, directions, or suggestions.
- Use an exclamation mark (!) if the feeling is very strong.

**A** **Tell the people to do or not do the following things.**

EXAMPLE:   Tell Lisa not to turn on the copier.          *Don't turn on the copier.*

1. Direct Marco to press the start button. _____
2. Tell me not to turn off the computer. _____
3. Tell them to wait for the phone call. _____
4. Warn Tan not to put his fingers near the shredder. _____
5. Direct your friend to connect the machine. _____
6. Tell us to record a message on the machine. _____
7. Warn Mrs. Kim not to answer the phone. _____
8. Direct Sam to enter a phone number in the machine. _____

**B** **Make each sentence negative, using the words in parentheses.**

EXAMPLE:   Record the new message. (old message)
                    *Don't record the old message.*

1. Turn on the new copier. (broken copier) _____
2. Put the paper in the top. (bottom) _____
3. Turn off the shredder. (printer) _____
4. Press the stop button. (start button) _____
5. Enter a number. (name) _____
6. Wait for an answer. (beep) _____
7. Connect the printer to the computer. (fax) _____
8. Place the paper in the top slot. (middle slot) _____
9. Keep the printer near the copier. (phone) _____
10. Turn off the copier at night. (in the morning) _____

## CHALLENGE 1 ▶ Review: Adjectives and noun modifiers

| Adjectives | Noun modifiers |
|---|---|
| Adjectives describe nouns.<br>    I'm looking for a **good** job. | A noun can sometimes describe another noun.<br>    I go to a **discussion** group at the library. |
| Adjectives come before nouns.<br>    She's going to be a **registered** nurse. | The second noun is more general than the first.<br>    The **discussion** group talks about careers. |
| Adjectives do not change for plural nouns.<br>    You have **big** plans for the future. | The first noun is always singular.<br>    There are three different **discussion** groups. |
| You can put two adjectives before a noun.<br>Use a comma between the adjectives.<br>    We plan to have a **long, happy** life. | You can put a number before a noun modifier. Use<br>a hyphen between the number and the modifier.<br>    You went to a **two-day** workshop.<br>    (Meaning: two days, not two workshops) |

**A**   **Rewrite each sentence using the adjective in parentheses.**

EXAMPLE:   I'm going to a school. (vocational)   ___*I'm going to a vocational school.*___

1.  We want to get jobs. (new)                     _____
2.  It's a change for me. (difficult)              _____
3.  Marina has a career. (good)                    _____
4.  She's a lawyer. (great)                         _____
5.  She has a home in New York. (nice)             _____
6.  She has children. (small)                       _____
7.  Boris is an accountant. (amazing)              _____
8.  He is also a father. (wonderful)               _____
9.  He has a family. (large)                         _____
10. They live in a town in California. (quiet)     _____

**B**   **Answer each question using the underlined noun as a noun modifier in your answer.**

EXAMPLE:   What do you call a card you get at the library?        ___*a library card*___

1.  What do you call a clerk who is at the desk in a hotel?        _____
2.  What do you call a desk where you get information?             _____
3.  What do you call a speaker who is a guest?                      _____
4.  What do you call a group that has a discussion?                 _____
5.  What do you call a diploma that you receive from a high school? _____
6.  What do you call a catalog where you learn about a college?     _____
7.  What do you call a school where you learn a trade?              _____
8.  What do you call a skill that is for life?                      _____
9.  What do you call a schedule for the bus?                        _____
10. What do you call an interview that is for a job?                _____

# Goals and Lifelong Learning

## CHALLENGE 2 ► Adverbs of manner

| Adjective | Adverb | Explanation |
|---|---|---|
| I am a **quick** learner. | I learn **quickly**. | Most adverbs of manner are formed by adding **-ly** to an adjective. |
| You have a **late** class. | The teacher came **late**. | Some adjectives and adverbs have the same form: **late, early, hard, fast**. |
| He is a **good** student. | He does **well** in class. | The adverb **well** is completely different from the adjective **good**. |

- If the adjective ends in **y**, change the **y** to **i** and add **-ly**: **happy** → **happily**.
- If the adjective ends in consonant + **le**, drop the **e** and add **-y**: **comfortable** → **comfortably**.
- If the adjective ends in **e**, just add **-ly**: **immediate** → **immediately**

**A** Change each adjective to an adverb of manner.

EXAMPLE: quiet ___*quietly*___

1. careful _____
2. hard _____
3. nice _____
4. angry _____

5. bad _____
6. good _____
7. noisy _____
8. fast _____

9. comfortable _____
10. easy _____
11. beautiful _____
12. nervous _____

**B** Find the mistake in the underlined adverb and rewrite it correctly.

EXAMPLE:  I learned English <u>easly</u>.  *easily*

1. I want to go to community college <u>immediatly</u> to learn computer programming.

2. I'm sure I can learn <u>quickily</u>.

3. I hope that I will do <u>good</u>.

4. In class, I'm going to listen <u>carefuly</u>.

5. I'm going to participate <u>happyly</u>.

6. At night, I'm going to study <u>lately</u>.

7. I have a computer and I can type <u>fastly</u>.

8. If I work <u>hardily</u>, I will get my diploma.

9. I think everything will work out <u>wonderfulily</u>.

10. If I have a good job, I can live <u>comfortablely</u>.

## UNIT 8  Goals and Lifelong Learning

## CHALLENGE 3 ▶ Review: Verbs followed by an infinitive

| Subject | Verb | Infinitive | |
|---|---|---|---|
| I | **want** | **to go** | to an adult school. |
| Lien | **plans** | **to have** | a good career. |
| We | **need** | **to study** | hard. |
| You | **don't plan** | **to be** | a teacher. |
| They | **are trying** | **to talk** | to the teacher. |

- An infinitive is **to** + the base form of a verb: **to get, to work, to be, to have.**
- An infinitive is often used after the following verbs:
  **want  plan  need  hope  like  love  ask  try**

**A**  Choose the verb to complete each sentence. Mark the correct bubble. Fill in the bubble completely.

EXAMPLE:  Ivan and Anya want ___ to the library.   A. go   B. to go   ⊙ A  ● B

1. They plan ___ books and videos.   A. borrowing   B. to borrow   ○ ○
2. Anya tries ___ two books a week.   A. to read   B. reads   ○ ○
3. Ivan likes ___ the Internet there.   A. to access   B. access   ○ ○
4. He also needs ___ the computer catalog for books.   A. searches   B. to search   ○ ○
5. They both want ___ the book discussion group.   A. to join   B. joining   ○ ○
6. Anya also wants ___ the creative writing workshop.   A. to try   B. tries   ○ ○
7. To take out books, they need ___ a library card.   A. have   B. to have   ○ ○
8. They are planning ___ again next Saturday.   A. to come   B. comes   ○ ○

**B**  Answer the questions using the words in parentheses.

EXAMPLE:  What do you want to do? (get a good job)   ___*I want to get a good job.*___

1. What do you like to do? (repair cars)   _____
2. What do you plan to do? (go to trade school)   _____
3. What does Ana want to do? (be a lawyer)   _____
4. What does Ana need to do? (go to a university)   _____
5. What doesn't she plan to do? (get married soon)   _____
6. What do you want to do? (get a bachelor's degree)   _____
7. What do you need to do? (study hard)   _____
8. What do you hope to do? (graduate in June)   _____
9. What does Habib want to do? (learn English)   _____
10. What doesn't he need to do? (talk to a counselor)   _____

## CHALLENGE 4 ▶ *It + be + adjective + infinitive*

| It + be (+ not) | Adjective | Infinitive phrase |
|---|---|---|
| It **is** (**It's**) | important | **to have** a high school diploma or a GED. |
| It **is** (**It's**) | fun | **to access** the Internet. |
| It **isn't** (**It's not**) | necessary | **to own** a computer. |
| It **isn't** (**It's not**) | hard | **to learn** English. |

• You can use an infinitive after the following adjectives:

| | | | | |
|---|---|---|---|---|
| **difficult** | **expensive** | **good** | **hard** | **interesting** |
| **easy** | **fun** | **great** | **important** | **necessary** |

**Ⓐ Circle the correct sentence.**

EXAMPLE: (It's important to have a degree.) / It's important having a degree.

1. It's not expensive go to a community college. / It's not expensive to go to a community college.

2. It's important to listen carefully in class. / It's important listens carefully in class.

3. It's good to participate in class discussions. / It's good participate in class discussions.

4. It's interesting to learns something new. / It's interesting to learn something new.

5. It's fun to talk to other students. / It's fun talked to other students.

6. It's not difficult to does well if you study. / It's not difficult to do well if you study.

7. It's not hard are successful. / It's not hard to be successful.

8. With a diploma, it's easy to get a good job. / With a diploma, it's easy get a good job.

**Ⓑ Use the words to write sentences.**

EXAMPLE:   not difficult / get a good job      ___*It's not difficult to get a good job.*___

1. good / have an Associate's Degree    _____

2. necessary / speak English well    _____

3. not difficult / find a school    _____

4. easy / go to a community college    _____

5. expensive / go to a university    _____

6. fun / learn about computers    _____

7. not hard / change jobs    _____

8. great / have prior experience    _____

9. important / work hard    _____

10. not necessary / be a U.S. citizen    _____

**UNIT 8** Goals and Lifelong Learning

## CHALLENGE 5 ► Future tense with *be going to*

| Subject | Future | Base | | Contractions |
|---------|--------|------|--|--------------|
| I | **am going to** | be | a nurse. | I**'m** |
| You, We, They | **are going to** | work | hard. | you**'re**, we**'re**, they**'re** |
| He, She, It | **is going to** | save | money. | he**'s**, she**'s**, it**'s** |

- Use **be going to** + base form to talk about plans for the future.
- To form the negative, put **not** after **am, are, is:** I **am not going to** be a counselor.

**A** Complete the sentences with the correct form of *be going to* + base.

EXAMPLE: (make) Mario __*is going to make*__ plans for the future.

1. (get) I _____ a better job.
2. (study) Marie _____ nursing.
3. (graduate) We _____ from the university.
4. (learn) Ilie _____ English at school.
5. (become) Miguel and Anita _____ U.S. citizens.
6. (not / return) You _____ to your country.
7. (get) My sister _____ married next year.
8. (not / buy) I _____ a house and a car.
9. (have) Many students _____ good careers.
10. (be) We _____ successful.

**B** Rewrite the sentences using *be going to.* Use contractions.

EXAMPLE: I have a new job. ___*I'm going to have a new job.*___

1. Ahmed goes to a trade school. _____
2. Lien is a counselor. _____
3. I need a part-time job. _____
4. We graduate in the spring. _____
5. Mario owns an auto repair business. _____
6. Martina and Ana study accounting. _____
7. We save money. _____
8. You work in a library. _____
9. I apply for a library card. _____
10. We access the Internet in the library. _____

Questions with *be going to*

## CHALLENGE 6 ▶ Questions with *be going to*

| Yes/no question | Short answer | |
|---|---|---|
| **Are** you **going to** study tonight? | Yes, I **am**. | No, I**'m not**. |
| **Is** Diem **going to** be a doctor? | Yes, he **is**. | No, he **isn't**. |
| **Are** they **going to** get married? | Yes, they **are**. | No, they **aren't**. |
| **Wh-** question | Answer | |
| When **am** I **going to** become a citizen? | You **are going to** become a citizen in five years. | |
| Who **is** she **going to** marry? | She **is going to** marry Antonio Vega. | |
| Where **are** we **going to** buy a house? | We **are going to** buy a house in Newtown. | |

**A**  Write the *yes/no* question for each answer.

EXAMPLE:  Q: _**Are you going to go to the library?**_  **A:** Yes, I am going to go to the library.

1. Q: _____  **A:** Yes, I am going to get a library card.

2. Q: _____  **A:** Yes, Lin is going to borrow some books.

3. Q: _____  **A:** No, we aren't going to watch videos.

4. Q: _____  **A:** Yes, they are going to listen to CDs.

5. Q: _____  **A:** Yes, Maya is going to listen to a speaker.

6. Q: _____  **A:** Yes, the staff is going to help you.

7. Q: _____  **A:** No, I am not going to go to a lecture.

8. Q: _____  **A:** No, Dan is not going to access the Internet.

**B**  Unscramble the words to write *wh-* questions with *be going to.*

EXAMPLE:  going / when / you / to / graduate / are  _**When are you going to graduate?**_

1. get / a diploma / he / going / to / how / is  _____

2. married / going / when / to / get / you / are  _____

3. become / why / is / going / to / a counselor / she  _____

4. who / I / going / to / the lecture / hear / at / am  _____

5. to / are / what / going / buy / we  _____

6. Tina / go / school / is / going / to / to / where  _____

7. children / have / when / going / are / they / to  _____

8. his country / how / going / to / Jean / return / to / is  _____

9. we / for help / going / who / are / to / ask  _____

10. when / you / get / are / a degree / to / going  _____

## CHALLENGE 7 ► Possessive form of nouns

| Noun | Ending | Example |
|------|--------|---------|
| Singular noun:<br>boy<br>Lien | Add apostrophe + **s.** | The **boy's** name is Joe.<br>What are **Lien's** plans for the future? |
| Plural noun ending in **s:**<br>boys | Add apostrophe only. | The **boys'** names are Luc and Diem. |
| Irregular plural nouns:<br>children | Add apostrophe + **s.** | What are your children**'s** names? |

• Use the possessive form for people and other living things: The **dog's** name is Spot.

• For inanimate objects, use **the ___ of ___: The address of the Adult Center** is 10 Main Street.

**A**   **Complete the sentences with the correct possessive form: 's or '.**

EXAMPLE:   Do you know what Ahmed_'s_ plans are?

1. I like to participate in my children___ school.
2. Lien participates in her child___ school also.
3. The girls___ teacher is from Haiti.
4. Sam___ school is a community college.
5. Our friends___ ESL class is on Monday.
6. Did you hear about Mario___ new class?
7. Sonia is going to be a teacher___ aide.
8. What are the men___ names?
9. When is the boys___ graduation?
10. The students___ goal is to get a diploma.

**B**   **Some of these sentences can show possession with 's or '. Rewrite these sentences. Write *no change* for the others.**

EXAMPLES:   The school of Juan is in New York.       _Juan's school is in New York._
            The name of the school is Wells College.   _no change_

1. Here is the library card of Tan.   _____
2. The address of the library is 29 South Street.   _____
3. The three children of Lana are in high school.   _____
4. The name of the boys are Bob and Mike.   _____
5. The name of the girl is Sophia.   _____
6. The name of the high school is Winslow High School.   _____
7. The plan of Marie is to be a registered nurse.   _____
8. The name of her boyfriend is Jean.   _____
9. Do you know the educational goal of Mario?   _____
10. Is the diploma of the school an Associate's Degree?   _____

## UNIT 8  Goals and Lifelong Learning

### CHALLENGE 8 ▶ Review: Possessive adjectives

| Subject pronoun | Possessive adjective | Example |
|---|---|---|
| I | **my** | I participate in **my** child's education. |
| you | **your** | Do you want to talk about **your** goal? |
| he | **his** | He wants to return to **his** first country. |
| she | **her** | She is going to get **her** GED. |
| it | **its** | The school has **its** graduation in June. |
| we | **our** | We want **our** children to go to college. |
| they | **their** | They help **their** daughter with her homework. |

- You can use a possessive adjective and a possessive noun together: **My friend's** name is Ahmed.

**A** Circle the correct possessive adjective that refers to each subject.

EXAMPLE:   Steve likes (his)/ my new school.

1. Lien talked about her / its plans.
2. You should get my / your diploma.
3. I want to get my / our Bachelor's Degree.
4. The library? It opens its / his doors at 9:00.
5. We're getting your / our GED in June.

6. Mario wants to have his / her own business.
7. They're going to make my / their plans come true.
8. I want to change our / my job.
9. You're getting your / our nursing degree.
10. The children need to listen to their / his teacher.

**B** Complete each sentence with the possessive adjective that refers to the subject.

EXAMPLE:   Lien is making _____**her**_____ plans for the future.

1. Do you want to get _____ Associate's Degree?
2. Ask Mario about _____ educational goals.
3. We are buying _____ first house.
4. Our dog's name is Fluffy. It is going to like _____ new home.
5. Anya and Ivan are going to get _____ U.S. citizenship.
6. You are going to have success with _____ job.
7. My sister says that _____ career is very important.
8. Should I ask _____ friends for help when I have problems?
9. They can give me _____ advice about school and jobs.
10. We are going to work hard and help _____ family, too.

# APPENDIX

## ► GLOSSARY OF GRAMMAR TERMS

| | |
|---|---|
| **adjective** | a word that describes a noun (Example: the _red_ hat) |
| **adverb** | a word that modifies a verb, adjective, or another adverb (Example: She eats _quickly_.) |
| **affirmative** | not negative and not a question (Example: _I like him._) |
| **animate/inanimate** | objects that act or move (Example: _teacher_ or _water_) / objects that don't act or move (Example: _book_ or _desk_) |
| **apostrophe** | a punctuation mark that shows missing letters in contractions or possession (Example: _It's_ or _Jim's_) |
| **article** | words used before a noun (Example: _a_, _an_, _the_) |
| **base form** | the main form of the verb, used without _to_ (Example: _be_, _have_, _study_) |
| **comma** | the punctuation mark (,) used to indicate a pause or separation (Example: I live in an apartment, and you live in a house.) |
| **complement** | a word or words that add to or complete an idea after the verb (Example: He _is happy_.) |
| **conjugation** | the forms of a verb (Example: I _am_, You _are_, We _are_, They _are_, He _is_, She _is_, It _is_) |
| **conjunction** | a type of word that joins other words or phrases (Example: Maria _and_ Gilberto) |
| **consonant** | any letter of the alphabet that is not a vowel (Example: B, C, D, F…) |
| **continuous form** | a verb form that expresses action during time (Example: He _is shopping_.) |
| **contraction** | shortening of a word, syllable, or word group by omission of a sound or letter (Example: It is = _It's_, does not = _doesn't_) |
| **count nouns** | nouns that can be counted by number (Example: one _apple_, two _apples_) |
| **definite article** | use of _the_ when a noun is known to speaker and listener (Example: I know _the_ store.) |
| **exclamation mark** | a punctuation symbol marking surprise or emotion (Example: Hello_!_) |
| **formal** | polite or respectful language (Example: _Could_ you _please_ give me that?) |
| **future** | a verb form in the future tense (Example: I _will_ study at that school next year.) |
| **imperative** | a command form of a verb (Example: _Listen_! or _Look out_!) |
| **indefinite article** | _a_ or _an_ used before a noun when something is talked about for the first time or when _the_ is too specific (Example: There's _a_ new restaurant in town.) |
| **infinitive** | the main form of a verb, usually used with _to_ (Example: I like _to run_ fast.) |
| **informal** | friendly or casual language (Example: _Can_ I have that?) |
| **irregular verb** | a verb different from regular form verbs (be = _am, are, is, was, were, being_) |
| **modal auxiliary** | a verb that indicates a mood (ability, possibility, etc.) and is followed by the base form of another verb (Example: I _can read_ English well.) |

| | |
|---|---|
| **modifier** | a word or phrase that describes another (Example: a _good_ friend) |
| **negative** | the opposite of affirmative (Example: She _does not like_ meat.) |
| **noun** | a name of a person, place, or thing (Example: _Joe_, _England_, _bottle_) |
| **non-count nouns** | nouns impossible or difficult to count (Example: _water_, _love_, _rice_, _fire_) |
| **object, direct** | the noun or pronoun acted on by the verb (Example: I eat _oranges_.) |
| **object pronoun** | replaces the noun taking the action (Example: _Julia_ is nice. I like _her_.) |
| **past tense** | a verb form used to express an action or a state in the past (Example: You _worked_ yesterday.) |
| **period** | a punctuation mark of a dot ending a sentence (.) |
| **plural** | indicating more than one (Example: _pencils_, _children_) |
| **possessive adjective** | an adjective expressing possession (Example: _our_ car) |
| **preposition** | a word that indicates relationship between objects (Example: _on_ the _desk_) |
| **present tense** | a verb tense representing the current time, not past or future (Example: They _are_ at home right now.) |
| **pronoun** | a word used in place of a noun (Example: _Ted_ is 65. _He_ is retired.) |
| **question form** | to ask or look for an answer (Example: _Where is my book?_) |
| **regular verb** | verb with endings that are regular and follow the rule (Example: work = _work, works, worked, working_) |
| **sentence** | a thought expressed in words, with a subject and verb (Example: _Julia works hard._) |
| **short answer** | a response to a _yes/no_ question, usually a subject pronoun and auxiliary verb (Example: _Yes, I am._ or _No, he doesn't._) |
| **singular** | one object (Example: _a cat_) |
| **statement** | a sentence (Example: _The weather is rainy today._) |
| **subject** | the noun that does the action in a sentence (Example: _The gardener_ works here.) |
| **subject pronoun** | a pronoun that takes the place of a subject (Example: _John_ is a student. _He_ is smart.) |
| **syllable** | a part of a word as determined by vowel sounds and rhythm (Example: _ta-ble_) |
| **tag questions** | short informal questions that come at the end of sentences in speech (Example: You like soup, _don't you?_ They aren't hungry, _are they?_) |
| **tense** | the part of a verb that shows the past, present, or future time (Example: He _talked_.) |
| **verb** | word describing an action or state (Example: The boys _walk_ to school; I _am_ tired.) |
| **vowels** | the letters _a, e, i, o, u_, and sometimes _y_ |
| **wh- questions** | questions that ask for information, usually starting with _Who, What, When, Where,_ or _Why._ (Example: _Where_ do you live?) _How_ is often included in this group. |
| **yes/no questions** | questions that ask for an affirmative or a negative answer (Example: _Are you happy?_) |

# ▶ GRAMMAR REFERENCE

**The Simple Present – *have***

| I, you, we, they | have | three brothers.<br>a cat. |
|---|---|---|
| he, she, it | has | free time.<br>black hair. |

**The Simple Present – *have* (negative)**

| I, you, we, they | do not (don't) | have | children.<br>a dog. |
|---|---|---|---|
| he , she, it | does not (doesn't) | | free time.<br>blond hair. |

**The Simple Present – *be***

| I | am | Gilberto. |
|---|---|---|
| you, we, they | are | a cook. |
| he, she, it | is | happy.<br>from Brazil. |

**The Simple Present – *be* (negative)**

| I | am ('m) not | hungry. |
|---|---|---|
| you, we, they | are ('re) not (aren't) | from Mexico. |
| he, she, it | is ('s) not (isn't) | a student. |

**The Simple Present – Regular verbs**

| I, you, we, they | wear<br>buy<br>want | shoes. |
|---|---|---|
| he, she, it | wears<br>buys<br>wants | |

**The Simple Present – Regular verbs (negative)**

| I, you, we, they | do not (don't) | wear<br>buy<br>want | sandals. |
|---|---|---|---|
| he, she, it | does not (doesn't) | | |

**The Present Continuous**

| Subject | *be* | + Verb + *ing* | |
|---|---|---|---|
| I | am | walking | right now. |
| you, we, they | are | sitting | at this moment. |
| he, she, it | is | writing | today. |

**The Simple Past – Regular verbs**

| Subject | Base + *ed* | Sentence |
|---|---|---|
| I, you, we, they, he, she, it | talked | I talked to the doctor. |
| | walked | She walked to work. |
| | played | They played football. |

**The Simple Past – Regular verbs (negative)**

| Subject | *did* + *not* | Base | Sentence |
|---|---|---|---|
| I, you, we, they, he, she, it | did not (didn't) | talk | I did not talk with customers. |
| | | answer | She did not answer the phone. |
| | | work | We didn't work in the evenings. |

**The Simple Past – *be***

| Subject | Past | Sentence |
|---|---|---|
| I, he, she, it | was | She was a cashier. |
| you, we, they | were | You were at a hotel. |

**The Simple Past – *be* (negative)**

| Subject | Past + *not* | Sentence |
|---|---|---|
| I, he, she, it | was not (wasn't) | Dalva wasn't a desk clerk. |
| you, we, they | were not (weren't) | They weren't at the restaurant. |

## The Modal Verb – *should*

| Subject | Modal verb | Base | Sentence |
|---|---|---|---|
| I, you, | should | exercise | You should exercise every day. |
| we, they | | eat | They should eat three meals a day. |
| he, she, it | | sleep | He should sleep eight hours a day. |

## The Modal Verb – *should* (negative)

| Subject | Modal verb | *not* | Base | Sentence |
|---|---|---|---|---|
| I, you, | should | not | take | You shouldn't take aspirin. |
| we, they, | (shouldn't) | | drive | They shouldn't drive. |
| he, she, it | | | eat | She shouldn't eat fatty foods. |

## The Modal Verb – *should* (question form)

| *Should* | Subject | Base | Sentence |
|---|---|---|---|
| should | I, you, we, they | take | Should I take two tablets? |
| | he, she, it, | call | Should we call a doctor? |
| | | go | Should he go to the hospital? |

## The Modal verb – *can*

| Subject | *can* | Base | Sentence |
|---|---|---|---|
| I, you, we, they | can | fix | I can fix a car. |
| he, she, it | | use | They can use a fax machine. |
| | | type | He can type. |

## The Modal Verb – *can* (negative)

| Subject | *cannot = can't* | Base | Sentence |
|---|---|---|---|
| I, you, we, they | cannot* (can't) | cook | I can't cook. |
| he, she, it | | drive | They can't drive. |
| | | speak | She can't speak Spanish. |

*Cannot* is one word.

## The Modal Verb – *can* (question form)

| *can* | Subject | Base | Sentence |
|---|---|---|---|
| can | I, you, we, they, | ask | Can I ask a question? |
| | he, she, it | speak | Can they speak Spanish? |
| | | use | Can he use a computer? |

## Verb + Infinitive

| Subject | Verb | Infinitive (*to* + base) | | Sentence |
|---|---|---|---|---|
| I, you, we, they | want, need, plan | to | graduate | I want to graduate in spring. |
| | | | study | We need to study computers. |
| he, she, it | wants, needs, plans | | get | He plans to get a job. |

## Future – *going to*

| Subject | *be* + *going to* | Base | Sentence |
|---|---|---|---|
| I | am going to | be | I am going to be a nurse. |
| you, we, they | are going to | work | You are going to work hard. |
| he, she, it | is going to | save | She is going to save money. |

# ► IRREGULAR SIMPLE PAST VERB LIST

| Base form | Simple past form | Base form | Simple past form |
|---|---|---|---|
| be | was, were | make | made |
| break | broke | pay | paid |
| buy | bought | put | put |
| can | could | read | read |
| choose | chose | run | ran |
| come | came | say | said |
| cut | cut | see | saw |
| do | did | sell | sold |
| draw | drew | send | sent |
| drink | drank | shut | shut |
| drive | drove | sit | sat |
| eat | ate | sleep | slept |
| find | found | speak | spoke |
| get | got | spend | spent |
| go | went | swim | swam |
| give | gave | take | took |
| have | had | teach | taught |
| hear | heard | understand | understood |
| hurt | hurt | wake | woke |
| keep | kept | wear | wore |
| know | knew | write | wrote |

# ► CONJUGATED VERB LIST

## Regular verbs

| **Base:** work | **Infinitive:** to work | | |
|---|---|---|---|
| **Simple present** | **Present continuous** | **Simple past** | **Future** |
| I work | I am working | I worked | I will work |
| you work | you are working | you worked | you will work |
| we work | we are working | we worked | we will work |
| they work | they are working | they worked | they will work |
| he works | he is working | he worked | he will work |
| she works | she is working | she worked | she will work |
| it works | it is working | it worked | it will work |

| **Base:** live | **Infinitive:** to live | | |
|---|---|---|---|
| **Simple present** | **Present continuous** | **Simple past** | **Future** |
| I live | I am living | I lived | I will live |
| you live | you are living | you lived | you will live |
| we live | we are living | we lived | we will live |
| they live | they are living | they lived | they will live |
| he lives | he is living | he lived | he will live |
| she lives | she is living | she lived | she will live |
| it lives | it is living | it lived | it will live |

| **Base:** study | **Infinitive:** to study | | |
|---|---|---|---|
| **Simple present** | **Present continuous** | **Simple past** | **Future** |
| I study | I am studying | I studied | I will study |
| you study | you are studying | you studied | you will study |
| we study | we are studying | we studied | we will study |
| they study | they are studying | they studied | they will study |
| he studies | he is studying | he studied | he will study |
| she studies | she is studying | she studied | she will study |
| it studies | it is studying | it studied | it will study |

| **Base:** stop | **Infinitive:** to stop | | |
|---|---|---|---|
| **Simple present** | **Present continuous** | **Simple past** | **Future** |
| I stop | I am stopping | I stopped | I will stop |
| you stop | you are stopping | you stopped | you will stop |
| we stop | we are stopping | we stopped | we will stop |
| they stop | they are stopping | they stopped | they will stop |
| he stops | he is stopping | he stopped | he will stop |
| she stops | she is stopping | she stopped | she will stop |
| it stops | it is stopping | it stopped | it will stop |

# Irregular verbs

---

**Base:** be        **Infinitive:** to be

| Simple present | Present continuous | Simple past | Future |
|---|---|---|---|
| I am | I am being | I was | I will be |
| you are | you are being | you were | you will be |
| we are | we are being | we were | we will be |
| they are | they are being | they were | they will be |
| he is | he is being | he was | he will be |
| she is | she is being | she was | she will be |
| it is | it is being | it was | it will be |

---

**Base:** have        **Infinitive:** to have

| Simple present | Present continuous | Simple past | Future |
|---|---|---|---|
| I have | I am having | I had | I will have |
| you have | you are having | you had | you will have |
| we have | we are having | we had | we will have |
| they have | they are having | they had | they will have |
| he has | he is having | he had | he will have |
| she has | she is having | she had | she will have |
| it has | it is having | it had | it will have |

---

**Base:** go        **Infinitive:** to go

| Simple present | Present continuous | Simple past | Future |
|---|---|---|---|
| I go | I am going | I went | I will go |
| you go | you are going | you went | you will go |
| we go | we are going | we went | we will go |
| they go | they are going | they went | they will go |
| he goes | he is going | he went | he will go |
| she goes | she is going | she went | she will go |
| it goes | it is going | it went | it will go |

---

**Base:** run        **Infinitive:** to run

| Simple present | Present continuous | Simple past | Future |
|---|---|---|---|
| I run | I am running | I ran | I will run |
| you run | you are running | you ran | you will run |
| we run | we are running | we ran | we will run |
| they run | they are running | they ran | they will run |
| he runs | he is running | he ran | he will run |
| she runs | she is running | she ran | she will run |
| it runs | it is running | it ran | it will run |